REAL
ACCOUNT
PLANNING

A handbook for developing Account Plans that bring about real increased performance and results in complex B2B Selling

Copyright

Material from ProAct Business Development LLC

Occasionally in this book we refer to some specific tools from ProAct Business Development, and especially in the appendices we give full examples of some of their tools that represent best practice. ProAct has given permission for readers to use these tools for their own personal use, but not to distribute these materials in any way, and not for widespread, systematic usage. ProAct will be pleased to discuss with you commercial licensing of their suite of Account Planning tools. Contact info@proactbd.org

Acknowledgements

I did not realise how many people would be involved in producing a book such as this.

I must thank René Zaldivar, CEO, and all my colleagues at ProAct. They have inspired much of the content and have allowed me to replicate some of their own material throughout and particularly in the worked examples. This 'band of brothers' has worked incredibly hard to put on outstanding learning events for many thousands of Account Managers across the globe. Running great training programs is hard work, but also a lot of fun, and really allows all of us to continue developing our own skills and knowledge.

In particular I must single out Tom Edwards who reviewed early drafts, Kevin Barrett who provided the most detailed review, and Tom Rose who reviewed a draft and made sure that the British English is acceptable to American readers.

My wife Julie helped more that she can possibly imagine, having to put up with me being absent for even longer over the last few months.

Finally, they are too numerous to mention, but the thousands of Account Managers that I have worked with over the years who have shared their experience and wisdom, allowing me to learn shamelessly from them and distil their knowledge, skills and best practices into this book.

Support

There are a number of resources, including additional articles and electronic copies of some of the tools presented in this book, available from www.realaccountplanning.com

Case Examples

What Would You Do ?

Throughout this book there are a number of Case Examples where the situation is described, but not the action taken. There are no 'right' or 'wrong' answers to case examples such as this, which are designed to help in thinking through classic situations that sometimes get clouded when you have the myriad amounts of data in a real life account. You can go to www.realaccountplanning.com/Cases to read a selection of model responses and to make your own comments.

Case Studies

A number of Case Studies are presented in the book.

All are based on real-life experiences, although names, and some details have been changed so that they cannot be identified. In a few instances actual situations have been combined to create a composite to better illustrate a point.

REAL ACCOUNT PLANNING

A handbook for developing Account Plans that bring about real increased performance and results in complex B2B Selling

Steve Hoyle

CONTENTS

Preface

Real Account Management: The most competitive, challenging and rewarding game.

I was recently at a hotel helping to facilitate the development and review of Account Plans with a client. It happened to be in the middle of Croatia, a beautiful country and we were in a small town that was deserted apart from our group, and also the Croatian National Chess Championships.

It was fascinating to watch how top players approached the game including the preparation and the emotional intensity involved. Chess is certainly a very complex game requiring a mix of cunning, strategy, intuition, nerves, a strong will to win, and according to Bobby Fischer, for some the greatest ever Grand Master, intelligence, concentration, analysis, memory and creativity.

However, after a while as we watched these experts at chess play their games we realised that really chess is child's play.

Consider chess:

- Involves only 16 players
- With only 6 types of predefined 'personality'
- You know exactly where they are today
- You know exactly how they could move at any one time
- You have only one opponent and know exactly what their position is and what they are trying to achieve
- 'Winning' is clear; everything is black & white!

Whereas Account Management:

- Is not black and white
- 'Winning' is not always obvious

- There are many opponents & sometimes our opponents are actually our allies

- Other organisations have a bearing on our success

- We are dealing with numerous players, who are all individuals and who can react in often unpredictable ways

- Our positioning with the customer is often unclear

- Generally the customer does not act as one entity

Account Management is a passion that I have had as a practitioner, as someone managing sales teams in complex B2B environments, as a consultant, coach and trainer. For me, it represents the ultimate in selling, and the ultimate in business. Yet there are many people calling themselves 'Account Managers' who do no such thing, and merely act as some kind of conduit between a company and its customers.

This book is titled Real Account Planning because it will only appeal to those real Account Managers who strive to manage the relationship with their account properly. They are engaged in an honourable, risky endeavour which can be immensely rewarding (in every sense) and which requires skill, concentration, a strong will, creativity and analysis when planning, combined with the skills to execute on your plan with the customer.

Real Account Managers are not simple shopkeepers who respond to customer requests, but they seek to proactively drive the relationship and business.

Chess Grand Masters are doubtless born with great talent, but then need to hone their skills and experience over time. The great ones are passionate about the game that they play, passionate about winning and being the best by continually seeking to learn more and improve their abilities; the parallels with great real Account Managers is obvious.

In this book I hope to present some concepts, thoughts and tools that represent best practice, sometimes from my own experience but mostly from observing and studying the great real Account Managers that I have been able to observe and work with over the years. Some of the content will be obvious, some will mirror what you see in your own experiences and hopefully some is new to you and will give you greater insight into this fantastic game.

The intention is not to try and teach the best way to develop an account as only the Account Manager can make that judgment. The intent is much more simply to give you a framework in which you can develop really effective plans to develop your business; I also aim to ask a few questions which are hopefully pertinent, to suggest a few exercises that most practicing real Account Managers tell me are useful and to share a little of the magic that I have observed in the most successful individuals and teams.

By itself the book cannot make you a better real Account Manager, but by spending some time in thinking about what it is that you do, applying some simple but powerful principles and tools and then using your own determination, creativity, flair, hard work and intelligence you will become significantly better at what you do.

By practicing and continually improving real Account Management and utilising real Account Planning you will become more in control of your business rather than your business controlling you.

Good real Account Planning and real Account Management.

Steve Hoyle

August 2013

PART 1: CONTEXT AND THE CRITICAL NEED FOR REAL ACCOUNT PLANNING

"If you do not change direction, you may end up where you are heading"

Laozi
6th century BC; considered by many as the founder of Taoism

"If you don't know where you're goin', any road will take you there"

George Harrison

Why real Account Planning

'Account Manager' is one of the most misunderstood and abused terms used in industry today. The vast majority of Account Managers are Sales Representatives or Customer Service Representatives. There is nothing wrong with these fine roles, however they are not Account Managers.

Most experts and academics disagree on the precise definition of the word 'manager' although most would include words and phrases such as 'leader', 'organiser, and achieving pre-determined results. They don't normally mean just responding to requests, phoning up every 3 months to see if you want to buy something, or sorting out any complaints that arise.

When we refer to real Account Management we are talking about someone who thoroughly understands all aspects of the business relationship that we have today, who has formulated a clear view of how they want that relationship to be in the future, and then has consciously chosen how they are going to achieve those things in the most effective manner possible. The effective real Account Manager then rigorously pursues these actions as well as constantly monitoring and reviewing the plan for refinements based on changing circumstances.

Real Account Management is a very proactive affair, involving business leadership and in most cases the leadership of teams (and often the more challenging situation of leadership without formal authority).

For real Account Managers, real Account Planning becomes second nature. They will naturally be taking proactive steps such as examining the relationships, looking for opportunities and deciding on actions to take which can either generate increased net new business, change the odds of long-term success or help the Account Team to become more efficient and effective.

Without real Account Planning, real Account Management is not possible, and 'Account Managers' become just reactive sales people hoping that their good tactics can win the day. Sometimes they may be able to meet their targets, but in the vast majority of cases only because they managed to negotiate those targets down on the basis of "my understanding of the account is that they are not going to spend that much". Certainly they will not be maximising revenues and profit from the account.

Account Servicing, Managing and Developing

One model that many people have found useful is in making the distinction between Account Supporting, Account Servicing and real Account Management.

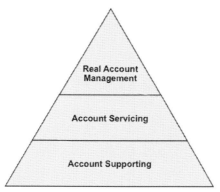

Account Supporting

Account Supporting is the first level of handling accounts and indeed a lot of good business can be transacted this way. It is the method mostly carried out by 'Farmers'.

- Mostly at the operational level (e.g. IT Manager)
- Focus on customer operational issues
- Fulfilling additional demand

Typical conversations are along the lines of "What are your plans to expand / change this solution?"

Account Supporting is still valid and valuable, but in today's world will ultimately fail if this is all that occurs.

Account Servicing

At the next level, Account Managers start looking to the future and getting involved in projects earlier.

- Mostly at senior operational (e.g. CIO) level
- Focus on functional issues
- Helping them to fulfil new solution demands

Typical conversations are along the lines of "What new solutions are you considering for implementation in the future?"

While starting to plan for the future and shape detailed requirements, this approach is still inherently reactive in that the initial interest and demand is being created elsewhere, by people that are probably being influenced by others.

Real Account Management

In real Account Management, the real Account Manager attempts to start driving demand from the very first moment, by discussing real business drivers, challenges, issues and possibilities with the people who will be creating the business requirement.

- Conversations mostly at C-level and / or business heads
- Focus on real business issues and improvement
- Creating and shaping new demand

Typical conversations are along the lines of "Let's discuss the changing nature of your business, and how different solutions may help you overcome specific challenges or take advantage of specific opportunities."

In real Account Management, the real Account Manager is proactively seeking to shape the whole buying process from very first inception, putting them in a far stronger position to be in control of future sales cycles.

An article based on this model can be downloaded from www.realaccountplanning.com/resources.

Why real Account Planning will be increasingly important

Selling is changing and quite dramatically; in particular complex B2B (business to business) selling is changing beyond recognition from the simple 1980's models that have been the foundation of most recent approaches. The financial crisis of 2008 acted as a tipping point for a number of longer-term trends as well as introducing some significant new factors into the way that people purchase complex solutions.

The New Norm of selling has emerged and is developing rapidly. It involves fundamental changes in how we approach accounts and impacts the need for real Account Planning in a number of ways:

- Relationships becoming more important means that we have to identify key individuals earlier and then proactively build relationships with them

- Relationships will need to be built outside of traditional contact bases (often technical departments and Procurement) which takes time and planning

- Increased governance and insistence on proper Business Cases will force all suppliers to become much more deeply familiar with their customer's actual business, rather than just the technical aspects of the solution, again forcing a longer term investment in particular prospective accounts

- 'New Business' in its traditional sense will become increasingly rare, as customers will want to develop a relationship, possibly involving minor projects, with possible suppliers before committing to any significant investment with them.

These changes will lead to a new breed of Account Manager as well as more focus on the functioning of extended Account Teams, who will need to generate (or at least buy-in to) a common

Real Account Planning   17 plan, which will also be used as an important communication tool with the wider supporting team.

Many studies have shown that customers increasingly want to move away from CAPEX based simple procurement models where they take all of the business and technical risk.

There is a proliferation of pay for performance or at least pay for utility models, complemented by the growth in Software / Utility / Service As A Service (XAAS). Typically in these environments the old 'big decision' followed by account servicing, is no longer appropriate, with real Account Management being needed to drive and expand profitable business for vendors.

The New Norm of Selling in Complex B2B

Many commentators have described the New Norm of Business since 2008; below is characterised the New Norm of Selling in complex B2B, driven mostly by the New Norm in Purchasing..

Relationships

It's about relationships, both personal and organisational. Business is so complex and inter-related today that making point one-off decisions will not work. Businesses are seeking longer-term true relationships with a smaller number of suppliers, and will expect them to behave in a responsible and mature manner. Trust is becoming more and more important especially as through increased transparency of information, it will become obvious when a 'partner' is not treating me as I believe they should treat me.

No more Hunters and Farmers

When relationships and trust are becoming increasingly important everyone will need to manage relationships. The old concept of the Hunter who can find new business and then pass it over to a Farmer who can handhold the customer during the rest of the relationship, is no longer relevant. Business relationships are becoming less about buying a one-off and then having it maintained for years to come. In practically all sectors customers demand suppliers to become more involved in providing true business value. Similarly, 'new' customers are less likely to respond to an aggressive sales campaign with people that they have not had a relationship with for some time. In the New Norm everyone manages relationships and creates, spots, shapes and nurtures opportunities in real time.

Propositions

Propositions will evolve to increase focus on results of business advantage. While relationships are increasingly important, at the same time customers are insisting on a relentless focus on quantifiable business benefit with proper Business Cases including detailed Return on Investment (ROI). Technology is no longer being bought 'for technology's sake' as business and financial decision makers and ratifiers are scrutinising decisions of technical recommenders much more.

Selling Processes

80's selling processes are becoming outdated. There are many people successfully selling complex B2B solutions today, who were trained and had 80's selling processes ingrained into their selling approach. Whether Blue Sheets, Foxes, 20 Questions or Flanking Strategies are your particular favourite, these approaches are in great danger of becoming outdated. They will continue to provide some much needed rigour, analysis and proactivity to the selling process, but at heart they are all based on Winning the Single Sales Opportunity (SSO), whereas in the New Norm the SSO will become much less important, and relationships (personal, business, technical, contractual, operational and financial) will play a much bigger part in business success.

New Models

New models are needed but industry accepted standards have not as yet emerged; in all cases though it is the Account Plan rather than the Single Sales Opportunity Plan that will be paramount.

Increased governance

Increased governance, scrutiny and insistence on real business advantage of deals as well as a desire to implement immediately are compounding the changes above as customers want it all tactically done today. This is an opportunity for strong supplier organisations that are smart enough to position themselves with the customer and ready themselves internally, so that they have relationships, structures, processes and strategies already in place to seize opportunities as they emerge. The ability to be agile requires strong foundation building in the first instance.

Myths and Old Norms

If you mention 'Account Planning' to many sales people they might respond with one of a number of old myths and statements born out of either never being educated around what real Account Planning is all about, or they may have been stifled by negative reactions of old time sales people, or even occasionally Sales Managers:

It will only sit in a drawer

Possibly, if the Account Manager is not a real Account Manager and just an Account Servicer, or if the company have implemented an inflexible programme aimed at the needs of management rather than the Account Team. In the great sales teams it is noticeable that real Account Managers take responsibility for creating and then driving some form of Plan, and they certainly don't wait for 'management' to force them to review a formal document.

Works only if integrated with the CRM

There are a few examples of where really good Account Planning is integrated with some form of CRM or sales force automation (SFA) system, however it is observable that in the majority of cases it is preferable if the Account Plan is NOT part of the real time system (although relevant information and documents should be easily available electronically to those people who have appropriate security access).

One analogy that is often drawn is that you would not want the company Business Plan to be integral to the real time accounting system, although some aspects such as targets may be embedded.

One of the key points of real Account Planning is that it is not wholly a real-time process; it requires and is based on standing back from the day-to-day to figure out what the relationship really is with this customer, what could possibly be achieved and then generating alternative strategies before deciding on optimal ways forward.

In the vast majority of cases where responsibility for Account Planning is handed over to an Operations or Administration type of group, the project will get initially well implemented, but will fall into disuse quite rapidly. Sales Management needs to own the process, which must be designed with the Account Manager and Account Team as the primary beneficiaries, with Operations or Administration heavily involved in making sure that it is well supported.

The Account Manager writes the Account Plan / The Sales Manager approves it

To be successful the Account Manager must take ultimate responsibility and ownership of the Account Plan, and will be heavily involved in crafting the content, however in the vast majority of complex B2B environments, the Account Plan needs to be a team effort, involving at least the core Account Team who are intimately involved with the customer and interacting with people who make or influence decisions.

Similarly if only the Sales Manager is involved in reviewing the Plan, then many opportunities will be lost, and it is doubtful whether the Account Team or the organisation will gain maximum benefits. Best practice is that a team of managers and other interested parties and stakeholders review the plan.

In addition we should be careful about 'approving' plans. Sometimes this is appropriate for at least part of the Plan, where expenditure or use of precious resources needs to be agreed. In general however the reviewing team should be there to provide context and guidance as well as coaching to the Account Manager and Account Team.

(In Part 4, as part of the section on Reviewing Account Plans, there is further commentary on best practice in this area.)

All Accounts need a formal Account Plan

This is simply not true and unrealistic; however good real Account Managers will be applying the principles of Account Planning to all accounts and indeed all situations. They will be constantly evaluating in their minds what the real situation is today, setting themselves some goals or objectives for the future and making conscious choices about the best way to proceed. They probably make some notes about this and they will involve others who are active in the account either in discussions about the 'plan' or to communicate it.

Only Top Accounts need a formal Account Plan

In some situations this may be true, but in most instances there will be a segmenting of accounts. Often the top accounts will justify a full Account Plan; in practice this will normally be a handful (most often up to five per Account Manager), which is the maximum number that most people can cope with. There will then often be a second tier of accounts where some reduced form of Account Planning is formally carried out, and as mentioned above, in all cases great real Account Managers are constantly planning (again see Part 4 for some best practice on Account Segmentation).

Account Planning is for existing customers only – handled by Farmers not Hunters

There are two dangerous assumptions here that can be dealt with separately.

For high quality real Account Plans a good knowledge of the customer is required, probably involving at least one 'inside supporter' of some kind that has been nurtured over time, and this will only be possible where there is some form of existing traction and relationship.

However, despite the fact that you may be missing some information and insight, it is generally a mistake not to have at least an outline long-term plan in place for New or Acquisition accounts. Indeed the cost, resources and time required to break in to new accounts mean that you should really only attempt a break-in where you know that they are a good longer term bet.

The second assumption built into the statement above is that salespeople should be classified into either Hunters or Farmers.

While it is sometimes best to have teams dedicated to new account acquisition, and behaviours in these teams may be somewhat different to Major Account teams, to classify people into Hunters or Farmers is lazy and does not really reflect what is needed to succeed in the New Norm of complex B2B selling (see above for an overview of New Norm Selling principles and rationale behind 'No more Hunters and Farmers').

Account Plans are only in place to satisfy Management

Industry is littered with examples of Account Planning programmes that have been put in place at the request of Senior Management, and designed to satisfy their needs for control, oversight, reporting, power, curiosity and because it is 'the right thing to do' or 'to protect the company in case you decided to leave'. In practically all cases where these were the only reasons for implementing Account Planning, the programme has failed.

Similarly any programme driven by the needs of Operations / Business Units / Finance / or any other non-customer interacting group, will be doomed to eventual failure.

Ideally the whole Account Planning programme should be centred on the needs of the Account Manager and the Account Team with the primary purpose of making them more successful. As a minimum the needs of the Account Manager and the Account Team should be given equal importance to the wishes of others.

The reason for this is partly philosophical; it is the Account Manager and Account Team who are responsible and accountable for the customer relationship (including revenues), so naturally they should drive the planning for how to develop these relationships. A more compelling argument is that for purely practical reasons the customer facing team needs to be fully behind the initiative and driving it rather than being driven by it. If not, then whatever incentives or threats are put into place by the organisation, and whatever support is delivered, after perhaps an initially encouraging start Account Plans will simply stop being used. The typical result is that six to twelve months after the programme is introduced it will be in a state of disrepair, with only lip service being applied.

Summary

- *Account Manager is a very abused term*

- *There is a big difference between Account Supporting, Account Servicing and real Account Management*

- *The New Norm of Business is driving a New Norm of Purchasing, which is driving a New Norm of Selling*

- *Myths and Old Norms are just that*

- *To survive, and particularly to be successful, real Account Managers and sales organisations need to embrace real Account Planning*

PART 2: WHAT GOES INTO A REAL ACCOUNT PLAN

"No one starts a war - or rather, no one in his senses ought to do so - without first being clear in his mind what he intends to achieve by that war and how he intends to conduct it."

Karl von Clausewitz
On War

"Real knowledge is to know the extent of one's ignorance"

Confucius

An Overall Model for an Account Plan

There are hundreds of templates and models for Account Plans, but at their heart the effective ones boil down to some very simple concepts.

The first thing that any good Plan will do is to define where you are at the moment, and describe the environment in which you are operating.

Secondly the Account Manager needs to look into the future and decide what it is that they want to achieve. Then they need to figure out how they are going to get there.

This approach always appears very simple, straightforward and powerful, yet is followed only by the few successful proactive real Account Managers.

When doing Account Planning, most salespeople do a reasonable job of understanding the situation, and indeed there are many 'account plans' which are primarily college essays about the customer. What the successful real Account Managers teach us is that understanding the customer and your situation is critical, but it is only the starting point for real Planning, which then looks into the future, evaluates options and makes decisions about where you want to end up, and what you are going to do.

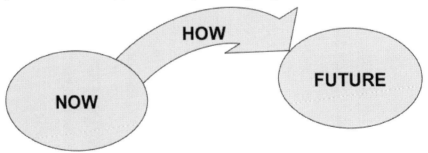

All three questions need to be answered, and different people might do this in different ways:

Now-How-Future: what we call an Incremental Plan; essentially this involves thinking of some good stuff to do and seeing where it

Real Account Planning

takes us. This may result in good but not great Plans as it will be increasingly difficult to come up with effective new ways of working, and the Account Manager can be limited by their past experiences. It will often leave you open to others (competitors and possibly the customer) blind-siding you with new, innovative and different approaches.

How: Many 'account planning' sessions are simply idea generating 'what can we do in this account' meetings. Again some good ideas may surface, but not grounded in reality and with no sense of strategic direction. Idea generation is a critically important part of real Account Planning, but needs to be done at the correct stage in the process, and certainly not alone.

Future-How-Now: Again we have all experienced lots of 'the Vision stuff' where generally non Account Managers paint a picture of the future that looks wonderful, but then discover too late that it bears no relationship to the present reality.

This kind of 'planning' is normally guaranteed to get seasoned Account Managers polishing up their LinkedIn profile or at best paying lip-service to the programme.

Now-Future-How: is the preferred method of successful real Account Managers. Understanding the Now, often analytical in nature, provides a solid and realistic foundation for the plan; indeed a good Situation Analysis will provide many of the clues for the future. Deciding on where you want to get to comes next as this enables the team to be realistic yet not limited by short-term actions. Leaving the How until the final part of the process will stretch you to come up with Strategies and Tactics that can meet more challenging Goals and Objectives.

Obviously in this process, once you look at the How you may discover that your original Future was too stretching or not stretching enough, so you may go and revise them in a very iterative process.

SA-GOST Model

While *Now-Future-How* is the overall approach, we need a little more precision to be able to put in place a real Account Plan which is succinct yet powerful and easily used and communicated by the Account Team.

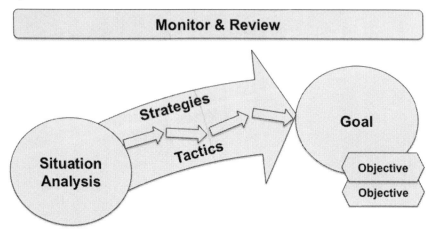

A more useful model is one where we talk about:

- Situation Analysis: describing the relationship today

- Goals and Objectives: describing where we want to be in the future

- Strategies and Tactics: describing how we are going to get there

The difference between Goals and Objectives is that a Goal Statement is a simple and descriptive 'headline' of where you want to be that is memorable and gives a sense of direction, while Objectives are very hard things that give precision and can be measured. Similarly, Strategies are broad descriptions of approach to achieving Goals and Objectives. Dealing in strategies allows you to have choice, whereas Tactics which are action items going straight into a To Do list, can be too numerous and too detailed to allow for effective planning.

A standard way of looking at this planning process is the SA-GOST Model. This is a standard planning tool, and can be adapted to suit the needs of the Account Manager by first asking the right questions during the Situation Analysis phase.

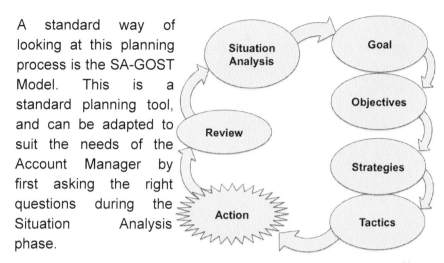

We have all seen many Account Plans that consist mostly of historical data about previous orders, installed equipment and services etc. This information may be relevant for the Account Team, but generally should be placed in the Backup Information to the Plan, because highlighting it in the main body will lead at best to obscuring the real issues and in many cases promoting a wholly tactical view of the opportunity.

Situation Analysis (SA) is how we refer to the 'Now'. It encompasses some relevant history and perhaps a little about the envisioned future environment, as well as solid information about the position today. It will include enough information to allow us to firmly ground our Account Management activities and planning, yet is succinct enough to be readable and manageable. Later we will go into detail about the three key elements to be considered for a great, sales focused, real Account Plan, together with how you can start to summarise the whole situation. In reviewing the best real Account Plans they generally examine three perspectives:

- The Client Business

- Our Competition

- The Playing Field

Situation Analysis: The Customer's Business

A critical and often overlooked aspect of good real Account Planning is to ensure that you understand the customer from their business perspective, and this doesn't mean that you simply copy and paste huge chunks from their Annual Report. You should interpret all the information that is available to you (publically and through private conversations) into a succinct summary that will help you in crafting winning strategies.

When reviewing an Account Plan, a senior manager will have a few questions that they want answered in the first one or two slides, so that they can start to understand the customer and the opportunity:

- What do they do?

- Are they successful – revenue, profit, EBITDA, market share, student numbers, number of patients, or whatever metrics the customer actually uses in their business. Are they getting better or worse (are the numbers rising or declining)

- How do these measures compare with others in their industry?

- What are the key issues that they face in their marketplace?

- What are their key Strategic Issues: the things that keep the CEO awake at night (as this will drive many decisions further down the organisation)?

- What are the key Operational Issues that they face in our area of expertise (lower level issues, for example, specialist functions such as the IT Department)?

It is tempting for some Account Managers to get carried away with this analysis, particularly since it is relatively easy to do by looking at publically available information. You are strongly encouraged to keep this section short and succinct as you are only looking for key trends that will affect your relationships and your strategies. If you have pages of data about the organisation, that is great, but please put it in an appendix otherwise you will burden yourself with too much detail that will make it very difficult for you to use the analysis, and you will likely switch off Account Team members and senior managers who are trying to help you in reviewing the Plan.

Similarly, some Account Managers only pay lip service to this part of the Analysis, seeing it as too far removed from the day-to-day reality of managing the account. These Account Managers are probably too myopic and tactical, failing to see that corporate top-level direction will have a big impact on buying decisions. For example, consider the different purchasing factors in:

- The major corporation, being successful in a growing market, trying to differentiate themselves on quality and innovation

- The struggling corporation, operating in a stagnant and price-sensitive market, who are only concerned with this quarter results

- The diversified corporation which has grown rapidly by acquisition, now looking to drive profitability

Often it may be that a major global customer should be broken down into smaller entities, and each entity approached in a different manner, especially if you detect different business drivers according to geography or product set. For example the tone in a division that is trying to grab market share in a high growth emerging market will be very different from that in a traditional stagnant market.

In some cases, where the account is made up of a number of distinct business units, it may be worthwhile to use some form of business analysis tool such as the famous Boston Matrix, originally developed by Bruce Henderson for the Boston Consulting Group in 1970 (simply Google it for many thorough explanations of the model). While the model which classifies business units into Question Marks, Stars, Cash Cows and Dogs has largely fallen out of favour with marketeers and management consultants, it can still be very useful for real Account Managers trying to understand the overall business thinking within different business units.

In summary, it is essential to 'put yourself in the shoes of the CEO' at some stage early in the account planning process. Ask yourself how does life like look from their perspective, as this will drive investment and purchase decisions further down the organisation, and give strong clues as to where to go hunting for possible new business.

Situation Analysis: The Playing Field

By the Playing Field, we mean that collection of individuals who are involved in decisions that affect the future relationship that we might have within this account. This will start with the organisation chart and include considering each individual in terms of their position in the decision making process, how they are likely to behave and how we might be able to influence them. The best real Account Managers will look at each person as an individual, and then consider how they play together.

Player Analysis

Understanding all of the 'players' in a purchasing decision is key to success. Research and observations over the last ten years clearly points to the fact that successful real Account Managers are very skilled at reading the people involved, and spend a lot of time analysing them as individuals and as part of the buying team. Typically answers can be easily supplied to questions such as:

- What is their current position in the organisation?

- How long they have been in this position?

- What is their background, including previous employers, education etc.?

- How are they perceived by their own senior management; are they a Rising Star / Performer / Question Mark / Deadwood?

- What is their previous experience of buying our kind of product or service?

- What are their career aspirations; especially what do they see as their next step and what they need to do to get there?

- How much risk are they likely to want to take with regard to our type of solution?

- How do others perceive them?

- What do they see as the key issues affecting them in their role today, and in the future?

- What do they see are the key issues that buying of our type of product or service are likely to affect?

- What is their position in the formal decision making process?
  - Decision Maker
  - Ratifier / Approver
  - Influencer
  - Recommender
  - Spectator

- How do they perceive us as a supplier; what would they say are our strengths and weaknesses?

- Are they, or could they be, our Agent / Inside Salesperson / Supporter; what do we have to do to create or nurture this relationship?

- Could they be a competitors Agent; our Enemy?

- How do they perceive each of our competitors?

- Who, within their own organisation, influences them?

- Who externally influences them?

- Who do they influence?

- How easy or difficult is it for us to get access to them?

In all cases, it is good practice to ask the question "why?" for any of your responses. For example, if they are an Influencer, then ask "why do they have this position, and why will they seek to use their influence?" If they perceive us as technically competent, then why is this; do they have previous direct experience of working with us, have we been recommended, is it our general industry presence or some other factor?

Testing our Agents

Having strong Agents (Inside Salespeople, Supporters etc.) will often prove crucial in securing large, strategically significant orders in complex B2B environments. Indeed many successful real Account Mangers and Sales Managers would qualify out any complex deal where there was not at least one very strong internal supporter, as they have learned from experience that it is normally impossible to win without someone feeding you inside information, intelligence and insight, as well as advocating and arguing your position when appropriate. Having participated in and facilitated literally thousands of Account Plans reviews, one major issue for more junior Account Managers (and even some seasoned professionals) is that they mistake an individual who is 'nice' to them as a true Internal Salesperson, whereas real Account Managers will scrutinise the individual and the personal relationship that they have, by asking questions such as:

- Why is this person our Agent?
- What will they personally perceive as a gain if we win?
- What will they personally perceive as a loss if others win?
- Are they passing us crucial information, intelligence and insight, which they are NOT passing to our competitors?
- Can we verify the information that they give us?
- Will they agree to some kind of joint plan or approach?

- Do we have demonstrable proof that they have directly or indirectly advocated our position ahead of our competitors?

- Have they shared their understanding of the politics at play in any significant purchasing decisions?

- Have they directly or indirectly introduced us to other people who will be useful in the future?

- Do they initiate conversations about future potential projects, or do they just respond to questions?

- Overall, do I feel confident enough in this individual to share with them my Account or Opportunity Plans?

While not having to have all of the above answered with a resounding 'yes', a good Inside Salesperson / Supporter / Agent will have positive responses to most of the above.

How they play together

As well as analysing each individual, it is normally critical to look at how they all play together, and the Playing Field will look at all of the people that we interact with, or could interact with. The example in Appendix 1 is typical of how real Account Managers would draw out a Playing Field.

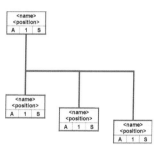

In this case the starting point is the relevant parts of the organisation chart, and then answer three critical questions:

- How do they perceive us as a supplier?
- How powerful are they (in determining choice of supplier)?
- How easy is it for us to gain access?

In this example the answers to each of the three questions are coded, however some people find it easier to use colour codes or differing shapes. Whatever is easiest for you to implement is probably best.

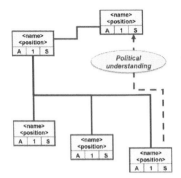

In highly complex organisations you may wish to go further and add in not just reporting lines, but lines of influence, specifying who has direct personal influence over others. This will enable you to start appreciating the more subtle discussions that occur for example who does a senior executive go to when they want some technical advice, or when they want to know how front line employees might react. Physically showing the influence lines is most often done by using different shaded or coloured lines.

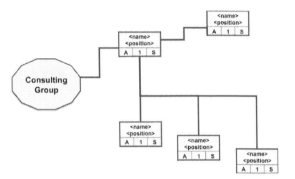

Often, with large accounts you will need a number of Playing Field diagrams to give an overall view of the situation, and make sure that you reference the linkages between them.

It is worthwhile experimenting with different forms of Playing Field to discover which is best for your style of accounts, or get a good external consultant to help you. A key consideration may be any tools that are available in your CRM or SFA application.

When you have settled on a format that works for you, then you should apply it rigorously so that it becomes easy to draw and interpret. Just as some technical people can look at a network diagram, or an application flowchart, and know instinctively where any problems may occur, the majority of real Account Managers and real Sales Managers become very skilled at viewing the Playing Field and understanding the politics of the situation very quickly.

Real Account Planning

Situation Analysis: Our Competition

When completing the Situation Analysis from the perspective of the Customer Business, you were asked to 'put yourselves in the shoes of the CEO' and look at the situation from their perspective.

Whatever your marketing department or senior management tell you, in practically all situations customers have choices, and in most markets you will have competitors who can deliver products and services which meet the customer basic requirements. It would be prudent to assume that these competitors also have salespeople who are reasonably good at what they do; maybe not as good as you, but people who have won deals in the past and who have customers (possibly including this customer) who quite like doing business with them.

Good real Account Managers, as well as putting themselves in the shoes of the customer, also put themselves in the shoes of their competitors. Specifically they put themselves in the shoes of the Account Manager from the competitor who is managing this account. This may require some research and also a bit of lateral thinking, getting over the prejudices that will have been built up over time.

If you can, imagine that for some crazy reason you have left your current employer and gone to work for your chief strategic competitor in this account; you are now managing this account for your new employer, and have all of the knowledge that you have gained over time about their customer. You could ask a number of key questions as the competitive Account Manager:

- What is the company history with this customer?

- What is our installed base?

- How many good Agents / Inside Salespeople / Supporters do we have in the account?

- How wide, deep and strong is our political coverage?

- What are our strengths in the account?

- What are our key weaknesses or exposures?

- How would we summarise the relationship that we have with this customer?

- If we were building an aggressive Account Development Plan, what would be the Goals and Objectives that we would set ourselves?

- What would be our Strategies and Tactics?

- In particular what would we do to put ourselves ahead of competitors?

- How does our senior management view this account and the opportunity?

For most real Account Managers, it is only through answering these questions honestly that they can get a true and realistic position of the competitive situation within the customer. This is needed in order to give us the clues so that we can construct a Plan that will keep us that little distance ahead. In a competitive market it is probably a collection of small gains that will make the difference between success and failure in an account.

Situation Analysis: Summarising the Relationship

Summarising the Situation Analysis is a really excellent time to take a pause from the planning process. By summarising you are trying to pull together and integrate everything that you have discovered or brought to the front of your mind during the planning process so far.

Doubtless, many clues as to what you should be doing in the future have already emerged and there is a big temptation to start writing down lots of actions for people to take. This might be a mistake as you will probably be focusing on short term fixes or opportunities, and your ideas may be dominated by actions that you have previously taken in other situations which may appear to be similar.

You may want to capture these initial action thoughts, as many of them could be useful, but excellent real Account Managers will hold off actually putting them into a plan right at this moment.

A good summary, using a SWOT Analysis, SWOT Plus, Relationship Evaluator or something similar will allow you to put everything into context and fully appreciate all aspects of the Account.

The most simple, and some would argue one of the most powerful is a SWOT Analysis (Strengths, Weaknesses, Opportunities and Threats). Even this simple tool has some variations and Appendix 5 gives a working definition for Account Managers.

Situation Analysis tends to be analytical by nature, with a lot of challenging and verifying of information. As we start to look into the future you will want to put yourself into a different state of mind, being much more open to new ideas, creative, imaginative and not stifled by what has gone before you in the account or even in your own experience.

When facilitating a major real Account Planning session best practice is to complete the Situation Analysis and Summarising on one day, and then reconvene either the next morning or maybe a few days later (but not too many days later when momentum has been lost). If time does not allow this, then at least take a break between finishing the Situation Analysis and starting the GOST future planning elements.

Goals

The purpose of a goal statement or statements is to give a clear sense of direction, describing the future in terms that can be inspirational and memorable.

Deciding on the Goal requires the Account Manager and the Account Team to project themselves into the future; to first imagine what might be possible and then deciding to commit themselves to achieving this future state.

Examples of Goals might be:

- To be the preferred supplier of all X class solutions to this account

- This account to be an industry reference for our Y type of solutions

- The most efficient and effective account in our region

- A trusted partner

- Our first $x million account

As can be seen, the choice of Goal reflects how we want to be able to describe the relationship at some point in the future. The Goal will be very dependent on what is possible, where we are starting from, the rest of our portfolio of accounts and what our product roadmap tells us about future opportunities.

A good Goal will be simple to articulate, paint a picture of the future, be memorable and appeal to all members of the Account Team.

Trusted Advisor / Partner

In many Account Planning sessions the term Trusted Advisor or Partner is often used. When quizzed some people really just use the phrase as a means of not having to think about what the relationship should actually be, however in general the sentiments behind these terms are genuine and powerful. *Real* Account Managers talk about how the terms imply going beyond simple supplier / customer relationships.

While the sentiments are good and indeed fit in with modern Consultative Selling approaches, with New Norm Selling and with real Account Management the use of these terms is now very clichéd and in many cases meaningless. In particular if used in front of your customer they could be negative, simply because they have been over-used in the past by lazy sales people who are just giving out platitudes. So the sentiments are to be applauded and encouraged, but please find different forms of your own words to express these sentiments.

A question that many Account Managers ask is 'How far out should we be planning?' There is no set answer to this but a rough rule of thumb is based on how long it takes to make a major change in the relationship. Examples of changes to relationships would be introducing new technology, changing the perceptions of the technical recommending department or perhaps breaking into a new division. In setting the Goal and the Objectives many real Account Managers would then double the longest time that we are considering. For example if we primarily want to be the preferred supplier of high end solutions in all countries globally for this account, and we think that this would normally take nine months, then we should set Goals and Objectives for the whole account eighteen months out, allowing for ramp up of activities, follow through and setting the next major activity.

In practice, for many technology or knowledge based companies, these types of changes are often between six to twelve months, and so they end up with account plans of between one and two years, which appears to be good general practice. In some instances going out to three or four years may be appropriate however it is rare for a plan beyond this to have much relevance, as the environment of technology, politics and relationships changes too quickly.

In complex Business to Business selling plans of less that twelve months are also quite rare and generally based on some event occurring soon that will bring severe disruption to the business and cannot be predicted. Putting effort into planning beyond this event would not make sense; for example the account as a viable business in its current form might be heavily dependent on renewing one of their contracts or licences.

As an Account Manager you could make alternate plans for each possible outcome, or you could simply plan up to the point of the major event, and then agree to re-plan once the future situation has been clarified (although even in this case, a good real Account Manager has probably created relationships, technical or contractual tie-ins and processes that would be useful in the event of any outcome).

Example Case: Mobile telephony infrastructure

Jorge Rodriguez had taken over responsibility for TotaCom, the country's third largest and fastest growing mobile phone operator. He was very excited about the possibility of selling next generation mobile phone infrastructure systems to TotaCom.

Having met with the rest of his team and been introduced to a wide variety of people at TotaCom, Jorge realises that he needs a clear Account Plan to move things forward in a coordinated way.

One of the big problems in managing this operator is that no one knew for certain if and when they would be awarded licences for next generation mobile telephony; TotaCom themselves were very confident in gaining the licences 'sometime over the next two years' and while they wanted to do everything possible to prepare, this fell short of spending any significant actual money.

Jorge also realised that while his company was well positioned technically and had good relationships with the technical recommenders, he was quite exposed as he did not have strong relationships with the eventual business decision makers. He would also not want to ignore the technical community as there is still quite a lot of good add-on, upgrade and services business to come from the existing implementations.

Faced with this situation, Jorge decided to create a plan that was unusual in having two major Goals:

- A short-term 12-month Goal of maximising this year's business, and positioning his company to be able to mount a successful bid for next generation infrastructure. All this activity to be self-funded with a checkpoint in activity when the timescale for award of licences is better known.

- A multi year Goal of becoming the infrastructure partner for all next generation services. The objectives would show a massive increase in revenues, with a major investment by his company probably in the second year but moving into profit by end of the following year.

Objectives

A single, simple to articulate Goal Statement (or even statements) is very powerful in allowing you to firstly debate and then easily communicate where you want to be with the account.

By their nature Goals can be aspirational, imprecise and difficult to measure against. This is why we need Objectives to sit alongside our Goals.

Objectives are very precise and give hard definitions of what is to be achieved. They allow easy measurement and promote absolute clarity. Particularly as business becomes more complex with larger Account Teams, often involving multiple partners engaging together in developing an account, the need for clarity becomes more and more important. 'Be the Preferred Partner' may be a powerful concept, but it means many different things to different people – a sure recipe for conflicts in the future if not clarified amongst the Account Team up front. Many people use the acronym SMART to describe Objectives, being:

Specific: defined in very clear detail

Measurable: a very clear yes/no test can be applied

Achievable: setting Objectives that are not achievable is a complete waste of everyone's time

Relevant: to the overall Goal

Time-bound: with absolute limits

There are many areas in which to set objectives, for example:

- Revenue received
- Orders received
- Gross margin received
- Sales of particular strategic products
- Pilot projects
- Approval / preferred lists / accreditations
- Customer satisfaction
- New accounts / new divisions
- References
- Resources used (cost of selling)
- Competitive knock-out

There is some work to do in turning these into fully SMART Objectives. As can be seen from the real-life examples below, they are not always easy to read, but pass the Acid Test of being suitable for payment of bonus against, where the decision to pay could be made by a financial controller with no knowledge of sales or the account (this is always a good theoretical Acid Test, but is not particularly recommended as a way of managing Account Managers).

Examples of SMART Objectives

- Obtain an official preferred supplier status, from group purchasing department, by end September
- Win 3 out of 4 of the following identified projects, by end of calendar year
- Obtain an average score of 9.2 from a representative sample of at least 6 people in this account in the annual customer satisfaction survey

- Both FD and GM agree that their projects can be used as reference sites, including that they can be mentioned in Press Releases, by end August

- We obtain at least 2 orders worth a minimum of 650K revenue each, from business units who have never previously ordered from us, by 31 December

- The frame agreement which is currently being discussed is signed by end July, committing the account to a minimum of 3m spend with us over the next 2 years, and with an incentive in place which makes it in their interest to spend at least 5m with us

- Starting in our third quarter, at least 50% of the business that we secure is for non-standard business, and this percentage increases every quarter for at least the next 4 quarters

- From 1/10, all business is won at a gross margin of at least 35%, and for next FY average GM on all business from this account is at least 45%

- Ensure that in the next 6 months, XY (our main competitor) does not secure any new project with a value of greater than 100K

- During the next 12 months, at least 3 projects of minimum value 350K are won where the initial lead was generated by our own sales activity, and which were not put out to open tender. (i.e. we generated initial interest in the business solution)

- Over the next 12 months we generate revenues of at least 200K every quarter, and at least 1.5m over the 12 months

Strategies

Creating, crafting, deciding on and moulding strategies are at the heart of the real Account Planning process.

A strategy describes how you are going to get from the current situation to your Goals and Objectives. It is a broad approach, and does not have to specify direct action, which is the job of Tactics later.

Because strategies are broad in their construction, you can be creative in coming up with new ones, you can debate the strengths and weaknesses of alternate strategies, and make proactive decisions about what to do and what not to do.

One of the tools developed by ProAct Business Development is the PROFT model for Account Strategies (Positioning, Relationships, Operational, Financial, Technical):

Positioning

How do you want the account to perceive your company; this is basic differentiation and key messaging. Are you specialists in one or a number of areas or are you a generalist with a proposition based on relationship? Are you the least cost or the highest quality supplier? Are you local or global? Are your propositions based on technical excellence or are they based on the relationships that you have built up?

Clearly your account specific Positioning has to be in line with your overall company positioning, but given that individuals in the account will describe you in a particular way, you will clearly want to proactively shape these perceptions. Positioning may also change over time, for example a break-in account strategy will often emphasise speciality in a particular application / discipline / geography, however once the initial engagement is secured you may want to position more broadly.

In developing your Positioning strategy you may want to ask some senior Decision Makers in your customer "How would you describe us as a business?" You would then decide how you want them to answer that question in say twelve months time, and what you are going to do to bring about this change in perception.

Relationships

Your analysis of the people and relationships in the Playing Field section of the Situation Analysis will often point to the fact that you are not perfectly aligned for how you want to take the account forward. As part of your strategy you will want to decide where to focus relationship building activities, priorities involved and the risks that you are prepared to take. For example you may decide that you need to build relationships outside of mid level technical recommenders, to focus on senior business executives. You might then be prepared to sacrifice some strength with existing lower level recommenders in order to be better placed with the business leaders who will sponsor new projects taking off.

Case Example: United Aerospace

What Would You Do ?

Sylvie Jenson is the ColaTel Account Director for United Aerospace, a European based global defence equipment manufacturer.

ColaTel is in a very strong position, exclusively supplying traditional telephone services across all of United's European facilities and being the preferred supplier globally. She is very content with the situation, having exceeded her target for the last three years, and forecasting to easily beat target again this year with a series of inter-linked projects from United.

Sylvie is however under pressure from her senior management to expand the business into new services that have become available over the last few years, particularly supply of data equipment and services. Recently she was given a directive that she should at least present the ColaTel entire product and services portfolio to all key decision makers in United Aerospace.

Sylvie is in a dilemma. Sylvie has had numerous conversations with her existing contacts in the IT Function and Procurement, who are very happy for ColaTel to supply all traditional telephone systems, where they are perceived as a 'trusted partner', however they have made it very clear that they do not want Sylvie to have discussions in any other areas, where they are equally content with their existing suppliers.

Sylvie knows that all is not well with all of the other existing suppliers. In fact she recently took a call from Basel Karanovich the COO of Maritime Surveillance Systems, one of United's smaller business units, asking her if she could quote for a new data based service. She has already sent him some general literature, however knows that she must keep a low profile otherwise her existing contacts, mainly Ken Sharpe, United's Global Director of Communications Systems, would be very upset at ColaTel promoting products that are not 'in the approved portfolio' and talking to user departments. In the past Ken has been very adamant that he expected all suppliers to have all conversations through 'the correct channels'.

Sylvie now has to make a decision, as Basel has invited her to submit a formal proposal, and has also invited her to meet with 'a number of senior United executives' and speak at an upcoming internal management conference.

Should she risk the wrath of Ken Sharpe and start building relationships with the business units, or should she continue with strong allegiance to the central function, protecting the current revenue stream.

What would you do? There are no 'right' or 'wrong' answers to Case Examples such as this, which are designed to help in thinking through classic situations, which sometimes get clouded when you have the myriad amounts of data in a real life account. You can go to www.realaccountplanning.com/Cases to read a selection of model responses and also to make your own comments.

Operational

As well as the strategic moves that you will be making as part of a real Account Plan, there are going to be a whole series of many and varied operational issues that will arise, and this part of the strategy deals with how you will handle the day-to-day requests, complaints, emergencies, and myriad other items that will get raised. Questions that you might want to consider include:

- Will you have regular internal account team reviews?
- Who handles special pricing requests?
- How will you efficiently deal with small quotes for add-ons and upgrades?
- Do you have regular reviews with the customer?
- How are service and support handled?
- What are the escalation points for customer complaints?

In many cases these type of topics are dealt with as they arise or become critical, whereas excellent real Account Managers will proactively plan on how to handle them.

It is amazing how often significant amounts of time can be saved, and customer satisfaction improved, by simply taking a little time as part of the Account Planning process and asking these types of questions. Additionally this area can serve to challenge Account Managers who in some cases will be handling all of the above types of issues themselves, as a means of staying in their own personal comfort zone.

Financial

Depending on the nature of the products and services that you are providing, there will be different financial relationships that you can have with the account.

You could historically have done business on a one-off project cost basis, in which case traditional Return on Investment (ROI) models will have been used, comparing a capital outlay with inflows and outflows of money over time.

Recently many customers are looking to different ways of regarding projects. ROI will still be used, but many senior business managers are less likely to want to take on the risk associated with large amounts of capital expenditure.

You can look to spread the cost of capital investments with different types of finance such as leasing, or provide some form of managed service, and even a form of risk sharing where your returns are based on the financial benefits accrued by the customer.

A financial strategy may be different for different projects although typically the financial proposition will look to get leverage by binding separate projects together, making an overall proposition more attractive, increasing stickiness and making it more difficult for new competitors to enter the account.

As well as the pure financial aspects, this is probably a good reminder to consider different contractual strategies, again deciding whether or not to tie together different elements with different timescales. This might be more attractive to the customer, but may make it easier for competitors to compete.

Technical

Lastly (and in most situations it should be the final piece of the jigsaw rather than the primary defining element) in the technical strategy you will decide the actual products and services that you are going to promote to the account, again taking into account acceptability, fitness for purpose, providing solutions to the customer business drivers and competitive positioning.

The detailed technical proposition may differ from project to project, but if appropriate, here you would look to define the overall architecture or preferred technology routes.

PROFT is a simple acronym for common strategy elements that many real Account Managers find useful.

Other Strategy themes

Other areas in which you may want to set strategies include:

Channel / Business Partnering strategies for suppliers to you or organisations that you want to partner with in the supply chain or influence map.

Service sales strategies in the majority of cases sales of service products should be totally integrated into your overall sales strategies, however in some rare examples it may be worthwhile to consider initial or renewal of services as a separate topic, particularly if your customer procures these through a different process or if you have sales people dedicated to these areas.

One-time services only strategies typically involving some form of professional services, where again there may be merit in looking at these separately as you will want to heavily involve the people responsible for delivery (Practice Managers, Consultants, Programme Managers etc.) in the messaging, positioning and selling of these services.

Particular product / propositions strategies again, in the New Norm of consultative and relationship based selling, we would not normally want to focus on particular products. In some cases however reality is that you may need, for sound overall business considerations, to focus demand creation or competitive selling of a particular proposition. This is often during the early period of product introductions where you want to gain traction in the market generally and within particular accounts.

Geographic coverage strategy may be applicable in certain cases.

Press Relations & Marketing Strategy will be critical in any account where you are either selling through (a reseller type arrangement) or selling alongside (for example a Service Provider who uses your solutions to meet their end user requirements). In a classic end-user environment this will include how you will use various marketing events to enhance your relationship strategy, who is going to get invited to what over time, and are you going to organise any special marketing or PR events specifically for this customer?

Deciding what NOT to do

Deciding what NOT to do is the test of an excellent real Account Manager. When we discuss Implementation of Account Plans and in particular reviewing Plans, then the question that normally is the most powerful is 'What have you decided not to do?' If you cannot answer this then you have not done any real Account Planning, you have simply documented what was in your mind – and probably what you always do.

Excellent professional real Account Managers will come up with many different strategies and make conscious choices between them, rather than just doing what seems natural. It is this constant challenging of themselves and their team that sets excellent real Account Managers apart from the merely good.

Tactics

Tactics are where your strategies come alive and are put into action. Tactics are where 'the rubber hits the road' and will define firm actions to be taken with owners, timescales and possibly outcomes specified as well as costs / budgets allocated.

Tactics should be detailed enough that they can go straight into someone's To Do list and be reviewed with a simple yes or no during account review sessions.

Most Tactical Action Plans will simply lay out:

- The action to be carried out
- Who is responsible for making sure it is carried out
- The time by which it will be completed
- Any outcome that is expected

- Plus perhaps some comments, where appropriate, to help the action owner and the rest of the team to be clear about what is expected.

Developing a set of great, hard hitting tactics which really move you forward in the account will be a matter of using your experience, creativity, innovation and the experiences of others (great real Account Managers tend to be enthusiastic stealers of good ideas from everywhere).

It is also an analytical exercise in that there are probably many actions you could take, but doing everything to every account is simply not feasible. Real Account Managers will explicitly or subconsciously evaluate all possible tactics against the difficulty of execution, which is normally time and / or cost, and the impact on helping to deliver a strategy that will lead to the desired Goals and Objectives. The best Tactics will clearly be very easy to implement and have huge impact.

In developing Tactics, you may also want to check:

- You are using the Account Team wisely and not all of the actions are owned by the Account Manager

- The timescales are realistic, in that they are achievable and will lead to meeting your time-bound Objectives

- They all integrate as part of the overall Strategies

- All Strategies have Tactics associated with them

- Are there any particular dependencies which have to be managed?

- Have you applied creativity and innovation, or are you simply doing what you have always done (not necessarily bad, but your Tactics can be a powerful way in which you can differentiate yourselves from competitors)?

- In reviewing the whole list of Tactics, can you combine or modify individual tactics to make them more efficient and effective?

- As with Strategies, have you decided on things that you will NOT do (the test of a good thorough planning process)?

An example of a tactical Action Plan is included in the ProAct MAP3 example in Appendix 1.

Business Proposition

By Business Proposition we mean the proposition from the real Account Manager back to his or her company.

It is generally accepted, particularly in the New Norm of Selling, that a successful real Account Manager will behave as if he or she were running their own business as a small subsidiary of the main company. Whatever reporting and remuneration is involved, having the mindset and attitude of running your own business turns out to be a strong characteristic of most successful real Account Managers.

The proposition back to the main company is at its heart very simple:

- *This is what I need from you...*

- *In return this is what you will get back...*

In this respect it is just like the owner of a small business going to their bank manager, or indeed the CEO of a major organisation approaching the Board of Directors with the overall business plan.

For a sales oriented real Account Manager, then the equation is normally:

This is what I need from you:

- Some of your time

- The time of members of the Account Team (presales, service delivery etc.)

- Some specific resources (normally time of specialist consultants etc.)
- Executive time (for Executive Sponsorship)
- Money (for campaigns, events etc. which are detailed in the Tactical Action Plan)
- Special pricing / terms
- Commitment to particular offerings (product / service features)

In return this is what you will get back:

- Orders
- Revenue
- Gross profit
- Other intangibles, often the ability to compete for other follow-on or linked business in this or other accounts (but a special plea to Account Managers: please avoid the word 'strategic' in your proposition; it is over used and will do you no favours with senior executives who have heard the word many times and normally when sales people want to give a big discount).

Where possible the resources requested will have been monetised and the whole proposition turned into a full business case, although in practice today there are few organisations doing this for anything but the very largest accounts.

The Business Proposition should make sense to any senior executive reviewing the plan, and a real Account Manager will have compared this proposition to others for similar accounts, and also compared against the norms that are expected.

Assumptions, risks, contingencies

In order to both help better understand the Business Proposition, and to put the Plan Conclusions into context, at this stage it is often useful to consider any assumptions, risks and contingencies that are inherent in the Plan.

Of course this section may be blank and totally redundant but often it is useful. Avoid the temptation to write extensively about all assumptions that your company makes in doing business or the global risks that you face; instead focus on the particulars of this account.

Assumptions could be about the account, your ability to do business with them or the external world. Assumptions are aspects of the plan that underpin it, and if an assumption were to prove unreal, then the whole plan would need to be reworked. Assumptions therefore are seen as very safe bets. Examples of Assumptions might be:

- The planned merger between X and Y is confirmed

- A third party continues to be able to supply a particular component

- No repeat of the major outage suffered last year

Risks are issues of which you are not so certain, and where you judge it prudent to build contingency moves. If a risk were to materialise then you would instigate the contingency, which might cause you to review and refine the overall plan.

Examples of risks and contingencies might be:

- The intention to merge with XYZ does not go ahead; *contingency is that we would downgrade our six month plus forecast by 30% and reduce resources accordingly*

- The third party is not able to supply a particular component; *contingency is that we can switch in another supplier, but some projects would be delayed by up to three months, however we can accelerate some background projects for a short period, to cover any shortfall in revenue*

- No major outages similar to last year; *if any do occur then we must be prepared to use emergency budgets to put in place a replacement system which will hit this year's profits*

Plan Conclusions

Having developed the plan and specified it to the level of detail demanded by a good Tactical Action Plan, the temptation for the Account Manager and the team is to sit back, relax and congratulate themselves on a job well done.

Clearly this is a mistake as firstly the plan is only a plan and will have to be implemented. Secondly, the plan can be enhanced very easily and with minimal effort, enabling it to be significantly more memorable, succinct and effective both for the team and others who will get involved in reviewing it.

Writing some conclusions on a separate slide or paragraph will force you and the team to really examine whether or not you have thought through all the issues that are relevant to this particular customer.

One useful tool that many real Account Managers use is the concept of **Critical Success Factors**.

A Critical Success Factor (normally termed simply a CSF) is one aspect of the Strategy or Tactics that is the most significantly important in achieving Goals and Objectives.

By thinking through and then stating the CSF's the real Account Manager and Account Team will ensure that they are clear on where the focus of activities will be.

Once you return to the 'real world' after having spent a short time planning, you will be faced with the normal torrent of activities that most customer facing people have in front of them today. When you and the Account Team are faced with mountains of emails, IM's, calls, meetings and a To Do list that stretches out forever, a set of simple CSF's will help to guide prioritisation.

In practice it has been found that having at most five CSF's will allow for sufficient focus, yet should enable coverage of the really significant elements.

Examples of CSF's might be:

- Gain higher and wider relationships

- Deliver the pilot on time and budget

- Develop joint business case process

- Evolve to a Managed Service ahead of competitors

- Renew the maintenance agreement for at least 3 years

- Turn Freda Smith from Enemy to Neutral

- Deliver an excellent proof of concept

The concept of the CSF is very simple, and its power lies in using it; try it out once you have developed a good overall plan to discover the power and usefulness.

Summary

- *Now – Future – How are the recommended steps for developing a real Account Plan*

- *SA - GOST is a well established tool to help with all planning*

- *Situation Analysis enables you to accurately understand the true nature of the relationship, and gives clues for the future*

- *Goals and Objectives state where you want to be; the real Account Manager has to take that walk into the future ahead of anyone else*

- *Strategies and Tactics define how you will reach your Goals and Objectives*

- *The process is designed to put you in control of your business, to really manage it, by giving you choice*

- *Deciding what NOT to do is a key attribute of a good planning process*

- *If you are operating this account as though it were your own business, then you would prepare a Business Proposition back to your own company: this is what I need, and this is what I will deliver*

- *A review of major Assumptions and Risks will quickly and easily significantly increase the plan realism*

- *Reflecting on the whole plan to determine Critical Success Factors is a great way of being clear on the key elements and to 'see the wood from the trees'*

- *You need to review the plan continuously, but from a solid foundation*

Real Account Planning

PART 3: DEVELOPING STRATEGY AND TACTICS

"The general who wins the battle makes many calculations in his temple before the battle is fought. The general who loses makes but few calculations beforehand"

Sun Tzu
The Art of War

"Ultimately, what separates a winner from a loser at the grandmaster level is the willingness to do the unthinkable. A brilliant strategy is, certainly, a matter of intelligence, but intelligence without audaciousness is not enough. Given the opportunity, I must have the guts to explode the game, to upend my opponent's thinking and, in so doing, unnerve him. So it is in business: One does not succeed by sticking to convention. When your opponent can easily anticipate every move you make, your strategy deteriorates and becomes commoditised'.

Garry Kasparov
(for most, the greatest ever chess Grand Master)

Part 3 examines a number of key issues that often are of concern to the real Account Manager and the real Account Team as they develop plans.

Points of Entry, Power and Pain

A simple yet interesting and revealing way of looking at a Relationship Strategy is to consider points of Entry, points of Power and points of Pain.

In many situations an account is first entered by access to a mid level technical manager or procurement person, who had an already identified requirement. They went out to the market to get further information or pricing, and either contacted a supplier directly, or were responsive when receiving a marketing call.

Alternatively when trying to break into a target account, the only individual that a salesperson could gain access to was the subject matter expert or individual directly tasked with looking into this area. These people may be in the Procurement or Purchasing department, or could be in the technical functions such as the IT Manager for IT related matters, the Learning & Development Manager for training or the Communications Manager for telephony systems.

More often than not, these individuals will be responsible for satisfying the demands placed upon them by others (their 'users') and while they may be able to make decisions about particular vendors, they will have to go back to someone else for budget approval or if they want to enter into any on-going financial commitment.

These individuals represent the Point of Entry into accounts. While they are often the first or only available contact point, they will many times remain as an important normal point of conversation and could well be our every-day contact.

We will have good discussions with them, they will make some tactical decisions themselves, and will influence or recommend more significant decisions. The thrust of our conversations (as defined in our real Account Plan) will be about the technical advantages of our product or service, compatibility with legacy or other existing solutions that we may have to co-exist with, fitness for purpose and price.

At some point in our account development activities we will want to get to the Points of Power, who have the ability to make or ratify large decisions; and in the New Norm since 2008 what constitutes a major decision is being defined by most organisations at a lower and lower level.

The Points of Power will typically be senior executive business management and increasingly financial managers. The thrust of our discussions here will probably be much more about satisfying the real business requirements as well as Total Cost of Ownership (TCO) of our solution versus others, and real Return On Investment (ROI).

Conventionally, Account Management has stopped at this point and successful Account Managers have struggled to cover all of the everyday contact Points of Entry for the various offerings that they might have, plus building and nurturing senior level contacts in the Points of Power to ensure that big decisions go their way.

Real Account Managers however go one stage further as they look to develop the account by creating and shaping future demand and being proactive in taking more control of business relationships and future projects.

Our Points of Entry and Points of Power are fine for managing demand from the customer, however they will not normally be at the forefront of creating demand. Our Points of Entry in particular while often influencing or suggesting new applications will also have a very vested interest in making sure that their department can deliver results in an easy and risk free manner. In many cases the Points of Entry and our everyday contacts are the ones who are resisting and supressing new demand in the account.

We need to seek out and build then nurture relationships with the Points of Pain if we are going to truly start creating and controlling demand. The Point of Pain will be someone whose primary job demands some change in how they go about things. They will typically be line of business or business unit managers with little expertise or knowledge of the products and services that you can supply, however they will have a critical business need that (maybe even unbeknown to them initially) you will be able to help them with.

The Points of Pain are the individuals who are motivated (or for whom it is a matter of survival) to go to the Points of Power to get budget approval (or approval to examine radically different ways of doing things); they will then go the Points of Entry who will get involved with the practical aspects of how the solution will get delivered.

Identifying the Points of Pain for your particular offerings will be difficult; your Industry Marketing colleagues should be able to help with generically whom they might be, but the real Account Manager will then have to navigate around the Account to identify the precise individuals.

Gaining access to them can be surprisingly easy, provided that you have a good, well though out initial business value proposition that can arouse their interest. Such an initial business value proposition will need to address a really key business issue that is causing them personal agony, now or in the future.

The conversations with Points of Pain will be about industry trends, their critical business issues, the impacts of these issues and how to construct a business case to gain the approval of senior executives in starting a project to address the recognised issues.

Account Development should be the ultimate goal of real Account Managers. To develop accounts will in nearly all cases involve going beyond the normal day to day and even senior level contacts (the Points of Entry and Points of Power) and generating new business requirements with the people who have the motivation and power to drive through the initiation of new projects (Points of Pain).

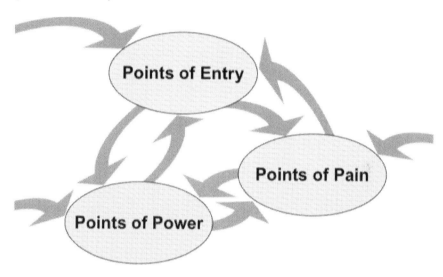

Case Example: VeloMore

What Would You Do ?

Michael Strong is an Account Manager for COMVIS a leading global supplier of telephony applications, and has just been asked to take over responsibility for the VeloMore account. He was apprehensive about taking over this account, which had been the company's top performing customer for the last two years. They are also the most prestigious reference customer for Contact Centre applications, which have been the fastest growing segment for his company globally.

There was a very large revenue target associated with the account, based on an agreed 'joint plan' with the customer covering the next twelve months, and so Michael thought that he could either 'meet expectations' and take the business that was already predicted, or something would happen and he would fail miserably. He saw only downside and no upside to taking on the account.

It was no surprise therefore when something did happen. The CIO who was Michael's biggest sponsor within VeloMore decided to leave just three days after he took over the account, and now it is two months later, and Judith Koops has been appointed as the new CIO. A quick Google search identified her as giving a reference quote for CCPeople, Michael's biggest competitor in VeloMore.

The 'joint plan' turned out to be no more than a shopping list from the customer together with a schedule of free consulting days expected from COMVIS. It was now meaningless, a situation that was confirmed during Michael's first meeting with Judith, which while professional was not warm and during which she had been totally non-committal.

Michael knew that he would have to do something different and needed a plan to get the situation back under control.

Looking through the previous Account Plan he realised that while there was a wide base of contacts within the customer, they were all either in the IT Group, operational managers within the Contact Centre itself or Procurement. There were a smattering of other senior executives, most notably Ken Davies, the Chief Financial Officer who had been involved towards the end of the initial purchase decision.

One strength in the relationship was with the Contact Centre Manager, Jim Larsson, who was a strong supporter and outside of Judith Koops' reporting structure. Michael arranged an off-site meeting with Jim to try and get some advice.

At the meeting in a local coffee shop, Jim confirmed that Koops was already having meetings with CCPeople and was trying to hold up a small upgrade order that the Contact Centre needed in the next three months.

Jim recounted the history of the Contact Centre, which was originally a part of the Customer Service organisation, designed to take inbound technical queries and service calls. They still carried out that function, but it had not changed much in the last few years, whereas the sales and marketing side had grown year on year. In fact overall management of the Contact Centre had been transferred to the Sales & Marketing function some two years ago.

Jim shared his view of the organisation chart:

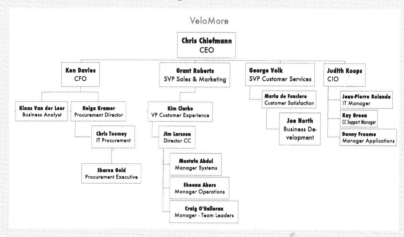

(see Appendix 6, for a full size version of this organisation chart)

Jim also confirmed the manner in which decisions regarding contact centre infrastructure were made:

- Overall requirements and long-range budgets were agreed with the entire business every six months and reviewed every quarter. This was as a part of the rolling 6-quarter consolidated Group Sales & Marketing Plan with which Jim was consulted but did not play a central part. All the various business units within VeloMore signed off on this plan, and from it Jim would work with Systems Architects in the IT team to generate user requirements.

- For add-ons, upgrades and minor enhancements to the systems, the procurement process would involve Jim, IT and procurement. For more significant changes to the system, final recommendations would be sponsored by Jim's bosses boss, Grant Roberts the SVP for Sales & Marketing, and would then have to go through the Business Project Approval committee, chaired by the Chief Financial Officer who would sign off on the final Business Case.

Jim told Michael that in his opinion he had strong support from himself and his team, Chris Toomey and Danny Froome. The people negative towards COMVIS are Judith Kools and Kay Green who is worried about her job. Everyone else was fairly neutral.

Michael had so far only met with Jim, Craig O'Hallaran, Chris Toomey, Judith Kools, Jean-Pierre Rolande and Kay Green, although Michael's predecessor had also met with Sharon Gold, Ken Davies and all of Jim's direct reports.

Obviously Jim had to get to meet with a number of other people, but the question that was occupying his mind was who to target as a matter of priority, and how to gain access to the different individuals.

What would you do? There are no 'right' or 'wrong' answers to Case Examples such as this, which are designed to help in thinking through classic situations, which sometimes get clouded when you have the myriad amounts of data in a real life account. You can go to www.realaccountplanning.com/Cases to read a selection of model responses and also to make your own comments.

Progressive Selling

The term Progressive Selling refers to a model that simplifies the normal sales funnel and relates it to the customer experience.

Unfortunately in the New Norm of Selling customers no longer wake up in the morning and decide to buy something; they go through a long and increasingly tortuous process. The latter stages of the process are relatively well known to everyone, and good sales force automation systems help enormously in codifying and making everyone involved in the selling process aware of progress.

But standing back from individual deals, a broader view of the process emerges, depicted in the simple model:

In B2C or simple B2B selling the 'relationships' may be through conferences, seminars, trade shows, publications, newsletters and advertising which are the normal way of having 'conversations' in these markets. In more complex B2B selling the relationships are more often one-to-one direct conversations where customers will discuss their business, their issues, their wants and desires with people from potential suppliers that they have some degree of trust with.

Out of these conversations will come Possibilities, when customers will be responding with:

- "That could be of interest"

- "We should do some form of quick feasibility study"

- "I'll ask one of my people to look into that"

- "I'll socialise that idea with a few of the people on the management team"

This is a crucial stage, and one where real Account Managers are busy in qualifying and shaping potential. Not all of these Possibilities will come to fruition as firm, well-qualified Opportunities, but those that do will have been influenced and moulded to your competitive advantage. There will still be huge amounts to do and many things that could go wrong, but as the creator of the Possibility you should be determining the momentum and the shape of the deal.

In good quality real Account Plans, you will see plenty of references to Relationships leading to Possibility areas, with strategies and tactics that would include:

- Meeting new people in new areas
- Introducing new application discussions
- Referencing new applications with business decision makers
- Offering to run small pilot programmes
- Sharing reference wins highlighting new forms of business advantage
- Unsolicited outline propositions and proposals

The alternative for many average sales people is to keep phoning around people asking "Have you got any opportunities that we could bid on this quarter?" Of course on occasions you are left with little choice if your funnel is for whatever reason very light and you need short term business. But it is a slippery slope where you get locked in to a short-term cycle of finding and then trying to close deals where you are never in the driving seat and have to respond to customer requirements that have probably been shaped by your competitors.

Developing Value for the organisation

As can be seen from the Progressive Selling approach, developing business is about using conversations to generate possibilities that become opportunities to be pursued.

But initial conversations have to get beyond the 'let's just get to know you' types of interaction. How long this takes depends on culture and many other factors; in New York City an Account Manager once remarked that it took 10 seconds before you had to start talking real potential business value or you would get shown the door, whereas in Rome some Account Managers will tell you that it takes three months and you cannot talk any business until you have had a long lunch together. These remarks were both meant to make a point, but there is at least some truth in them.

Much thought and planning can go into early stage conversations designed to plant seeds that have a good chance of flourishing. Most successful real Account Managers will go through a process of defining the potential value that they can add to an organisation, well before these types of conversations. The process of developing possible value propositions can be informal and unstructured, or increasingly it is carried out with a small team in a short facilitated workshop. There are many detailed processes that you can go through, but typically the steps involved would include:

1. Examining in detail the organisation's high level Business Imperatives; these would be the 'things that keep the CEO awake at night' as they will drive behaviour across the organisation. They will set the direction and frame much of the high level organisational decision making and could be things such as:

   • Increase market share

   • Rightsize the business

   • Improve the Balance Sheet for a pending sell-off

- Move from a product to a service based organisation
- Improve image and reputation in the marketplace

2. Look at how these high level Business Imperatives get translated into Operational Imperatives for the parts of the business that you are working with. Again, you can ask "what keeps this Business Unit Head awake at night", or "what keeps the Functional Manager (for example the CIO) awake at night?" In practice you will often have to ask both of the above questions where your offerings dissect for example both a Business Unit and a Functional Unit. Operational Imperatives might be issues such as:

- 10% efficiency gains year-on-year
- Reduce time to market
- Increase adaptability of the workforce
- Increase net promoter score by 15%
- Reduce churn by 20%

Clearly, there could be a number of levels of Operational Imperatives, and most real Account Managers will look at all levels which are involved in any way in influencing any potential project.

3. Generating, spotting and developing value is then a question of working through how your products or services could significantly impact the Business and Operational Imperatives, especially in ways that competitive products or services would struggle.

This kind of analysis and planning needs to be done with some rigour so that it provides clear signals as to the conversations that should be had to generate value-based demand, which you are in a strong position to fulfil. From this analysis however should come some clear Strategy Statements for areas to focus on to develop strong pipeline for the future.

Developing Value for the individual

Just as a rigorous analysis of organisational imperatives at the high level Business and Operational levels will enable you to form strong business-led value creation strategies, the same approach can be applied at the individual level.

In essence a good real Account Manager will take the analysis down to the personal level for any key individual that has been identified. The process would again start by considering the question 'what keeps this individual awake at night, in terms of their particular individual situation?'

Everyone in any organisation will have their own personal agenda, which might include desires for:

- A quiet life
- Avoiding (or getting) redundancy
- Making a name for themselves
- Earning increased bonus
- Being liked by colleagues
- Competing against others
- Receiving promotion

This kind of analysis of personal agendas is often only considered as part of the tactics of complex B2B selling, however analysing hundreds of lost sales and accounts where dominance was lost to a competitor indicates that a common strategic failing is in not aligning value creation demand generation with both Business and Personal Imperatives.

In crafting account development strategies it is vital to formulate approaches that tie together these two aspects. The resultant strategy statements might be along the lines of:

Focus demand creation activities on our range of packages that enable in depth reporting of customer attitudes *(rationale: aligned against their strategic direction of becoming more customer focused, the Sales Imperative of improving customer segmentation and the CIO need to be seen as an innovator supporting the business).*

Solution Development

While value creation normally starts by analysing customer Imperatives at different levels of the organisation, a different and complementary approach is Solution Mapping, where the starting point is the product or service that you are looking to introduce or expand in the account, and then working backwards to analyse who you should talk to about what issues in order to generate demand.

Clearly in a proactive real Account Management role within a complex B2B environment we would normally not be trying to 'sell' on a product or transactional basis, however there are often times where for good business reasons we wish to focus on demand generation of a particular product or service. We do not explicitly start 'pushing' this product, but seek to discover individuals with sufficient motivation to want to champion the kind of solution that we are able to supply (and clearly in a way where we have some competitive advantage).

One method of crafting your strategies for generating demand for a particular product or service is Solution Mapping. This takes a number of forms, but at the most simple level involves:

1. Being clear on what your solution can do

2. Being clear on what this means to a customer (the possible business benefits); ideally narrowing this down to a particular type of customer is a specific market, for example 'medium sized speciality retailers'

3. Expressing these benefits in terms of the problems that they solve

4. Mapping out whom in an organisation might see these as very serious problems to be solved. It turns out that for most of us, it is more productive to think in generalised terms initially, and then to be specific about our particular account as this tends to increase creativity without being hampered by our own probably narrow view of the particular customer

5. Determining how we can approach these individuals, including what can we use to gain immediate resonance with them

6. Putting in an action plan to make these contacts and start planting seeds about how we can solve particular significant problems that they might have

Solution Development Example

Imagine that you are looking to create demand for a new highly flexible and remote video surveillance solution into the retail market.

What the solution does:

- Enables monitoring of large areas, 24*7 in a highly flexible manner so that you are able to monitor a whole estate to a good level and then rapidly create more coverage into areas of particular interest.

Problems that it solves:

- High rates of vandalism
- Property damage and pilfering in stores
- Impacting store profit levels
- Security and perceived security of shoppers and resulting image and reputational issues.
- Similar security concerns of staff and resulting morale issues.

Who might perceive these as critical issues (who is kept awake worrying about these)

- Property damage, vandalism and pilfering in stores: Store Managers, Security company, Finance Director
- Security and perceived security of shoppers and resulting image and reputational issues: Store Manager, Marketing Manager, Security company
- Security concerns of staff and resulting morale issues: Store Managers, Human Resources, Trades Unions

Alternate strategies: your strategy could be one or a combination of:

- Approaching Store Managers directly with a multi-faceted solution *(possible, but difficult to access them directly and to get them to put this high on their list of priorities)*

- Working with existing contacts in IT to put forward an unsolicited proposal to Store Managers and Finance Directors *(easier to access them, but still have difficulty of how important this is to them; possibly use this as a secondary strategy once a champion has been nurtured through a different route)*

- Approaching Security companies *(possible, but they are mostly targeted by competition who are entrenched and we may find it hard to differentiate ourselves sufficiently)*

- Approaching Marketing *(possible, but this is not probably high on their list of priorities)*

- Approaching HR *(possible – easy to identify, but notoriously difficult to get an audience with)*

- Approaching Trades Unions *(possible; easy to identify and possible champions who can easily make this a higher priority issue for others, but we will need to follow up with internal sponsorship)*

Which of these is the optimal strategy will depend on your particular circumstances, further evaluation of where your competitors are approaching, ease of access to people and further judging of the extent of the problem to individuals.

In this example a possible strategy would be to approach Trades Unions with the object of getting this raised as a real issue, followed by working with existing IT contacts to showcase options and solutions to Store Managers.

The above is a simple example of what is often called Solution Mapping, a process best facilitated by an external consultant who can guide the sales team or real Account Manager in thinking broadly and then specifically through a process to craft strong action plans for generating business around a particular solution set within specific accounts.

Player Mapping

Player Mapping is normally regarded as a part of the Tactical Action Plan, and simply sets out the one-to-one personal relationships that you will seek to develop. It is an extension of and detail for an overall personal relationships strategy that you will have developed.

It is often the case that individual relationships develop haphazardly, especially during the early stages of account development, where simply gaining access to individuals is perhaps the key imperative.

An example simple Player Map is shown as part of the MAP3 example Account Plan in Appendix 1.

In the most basic form you list all of the individuals who you have contact with in the account, together with those whom you are likely to have contact with and those that you desire to meet immediately or at some stage in the future. You then match them up with individuals in your own organisation as their primary contact. This is the individual who should take a special interest in that individual, who the Account Manager can go to if they need information about the person, and who will seek to develop the relationship in line with the real Account Plan.

Naturally you will map together people based on areas of interest, perceived seniority (peering) and personality fit. For example a Pre-Sales Specialist may be mapped to Technical Recommenders, while a CEO may be mapped to one of your appropriate General Managers. You will also make sure that, for example, very focused and task oriented people are matched with people of a similar style.

Taking the time to construct the Player Map is often extremely valuable, and points that you may want to bear in mind are:

- Who are you missing a relationship with?

- Is the Account Manager holding too many of the personal relationships and could others manage them more effectively?

- Should you be keeping some of your senior management 'in reserve' to develop relationships with their peers at some stage in the future? (Often we find that senior management are used too early in an account relationship to help secure some particular tactical order or resolve a particular issue, however they then become locked in at a relatively low level)

- Is there clarity as to how we want to change perceptions of particular individuals?

- Are there particular individuals in the customer map who have multiple deep relationships within your own company, and is this a strength or the opportunity for mixed messaging and disjointed actions?

- Is everyone in the Account Team assisting in getting optimal coverage of all individuals?

Executive Sponsorship Programme

Many organisations have an Executive Sponsorship Programme, some of which are excellent but with many paying lip service to the concept. Often senior managers are simply assigned to accounts where they might have the occasional meeting but add little real value to the overall relationship.

Using senior executives wisely should be a key part of any good real Account Plan and in practice, real Account Managers make conscious decisions to either implement a good corporate programme or develop their own version appropriate to the account.

The aims of using or defining an Executive Sponsor Programme within the account can be many and varied, but might include:

- Gaining access to particular individuals that are difficult or impossible for the Account Manager to approach directly, because of hierarchy or functional titles. For example a busy VP of Marketing might be more likely to respond to a meeting with your senior Marketing Executive

- Independent coaching and mentoring of the Account Manager and Account Team, which may be difficult for line managers to carry out

- Uncovering new potential areas for business development through specialised knowledge or skills. For example a Director responsible for sales into Financial Services markets may understand industry trends much better than an Account Manager, and be able to search out and plant the seeds for new applications

- Providing an escalation point for senior customer executives both as part of normal channels, and also as an informal back channel

While such programmes come in various guises, in general the better ones have the following characteristics:

- Senior Executives must be fully committed to the role for the long haul; commitment for a minimum of two years would be normal, and time committed on a sustainable and regular basis

- Account Managers must be fully committed to the programme, in particular to involving and keeping the Executive informed at all appropriate times

- Agreement of the Senior Executive to operate and behave within the Account Plan, and to fully represent senior management across the whole organisation and not just representing their particular function

- Full briefings and debriefings given by / to the Account Manager with the active involvement of the Senior Executive at all times

- The full involvement of the Executive in guiding, developing, coaching and reviewing the Account Plan with the Account Team

Nurturing Agents

As discussed elsewhere, finding Agents (sometimes called Inside Salespeople or Supporters) is normally crucial to our success in any account as these are the individuals who give us good verifiable information that is not available to others and who will also advocate our position when appropriate and necessary.

We have already looked in the Situation Analysis at how we can test out if someone really is an Agent and when considering our strategy and tactics we need to look into how we can strengthen and nurture these Agents.

The key to this will be in understanding 'what's in it for me?' from the perspective of the Agent; why are they willing and enthusiastic in supporting us?

To help in this it may be useful to look at what motivates individuals to do anything, and fortunately there is a lot of research into this field that we can draw upon from classic figures such as

Abraham Maslow and Frederic Herzberg, to more recent researchers such as Robert Wubbolding and William Glasse. To paraphrase all of this type of work, and put it into our context of looking at what drives an Agent to support us, then there are a number of reasons:

- **Preserving their power** based on our solutions leading to an increase in the knowledge or skills based power that they already have; this is a common reason why incumbent suppliers have an in-built advantage, particularly where specialist skills or knowledge are required to effectively implement particular technology or services.

- **My enemy's enemy is my friend** is often true where there are competing political power plays, for example between competing business units, or between a business unit and a group wide technical or procurement function. This is often the case when we identify an Agent in an account that we are trying to break into against a strong incumbent.

- **Trust** we know is a key component in any purchasing decision, but can only be built up over time with individuals and with an organisation. The knowledge that on previous occasions this individual or organisation has helped me out of particular issues, and behaved in a professional manner gives me the confidence to want to support them in the future.

- **A Sense of Belonging** is often allied to Trust, where the bond is at a much more personal level, where the Agent has a natural affinity with the organisation and the individual, probably brought about by many instances of working hard together and socialising together. This is where the long nights sorting out problems and the time put into customer entertaining really pay off.

For some organisations, a Sense of Belonging is much more explicit. Companies such as Apple for example consciously create the feeling of inclusivity and the adoption of their technology being a part of a greater movement or outlook on life. Whether they do this through a sense of wanting to achieve greater good, or for pure marketing reasons is the subject of a different debate, however it certainly helps with recruiting and nurturing Agents.

- *Involvement* is again often allied to a Sense of Belonging. Agents tend to be much stronger when you both take them into your confidence and openly work with them to mutual advantage. Joint Planning can be a good tool in this respect (in addition to the actual plan that is produced) because the Agent takes ownership for the actions agreed.

- *Personal enhancement* is support based on the perception that explicitly gaining experience of working with a particular supplier will lead to some future career gain. For example many technical people in the 1990's wanted to gain Cisco experience to put on their CV.

The list above is not exhaustive and in reality it is often a combination of factors that apply. Each individual case will be different, and each person treated in a unique manner, however understanding which combination of the above factors is relevant in each individual case will help in crafting a strategy and tactics as to how to nurture an Agent.

Depending on the motivations of your Agent you will craft a nurturing strategy that will strengthen the relationship. The strategies and tactics available to you include the normal corporate entertaining, but you might also consider:

- Sitting on customer advisory councils (commercial or technical)
- Public speaking at customer events
- Visits to factory / R&D sites
- Access to key personnel, individually or at round tables

- Advance information about products / service / commercial changes

- Supporting their particular charities

- Giving them credit for project successes

- Beta testing new offerings

- Sponsorship / support onto industry bodies

- Sponsorship / support in industry awards

- Joint press releases

- Prioritising service and support calls

The list is endless, and while some may be subject to a view of business ethics by yourself and your organisation, you can apply a lot of creativity in generating approaches that are appropriate and powerful.

In addition to these explicit activities, even more powerful will be how you structure offers and deals so that they meet their own personal agendas (as well as your agenda).

The two questions to keep asking yourself are:

- Why is this individual supporting me / my company?

- What would they really value that will increase this support?

Case Example: Rucker & Willems

What Would You Do ?

You are an Account Manager with TotalMan Software Systems, a global vendor of time and billing applications. You are responsible for Rucker & Willems a successful management consulting company operating across the USA with some International operations.

Rucker & Willems has shown good growth over the last twelve years, through organic growth plus some acquisitions of smaller, regionally based operations. The firm focuses mainly on the needs of medium sized businesses and offers a broad range of services to their clients, with a proposition of being the 'one stop shop' for all consulting services at a reasonable cost.

Charlie Walker is Chief Technology Officer for the firm and is responsible for ensuring that all investments in technology are made in the best overall interests of the company. Charlie's role is a co-ordinating one as formal responsibility for most decisions rests with the powerful and quite autonomous Operating Units, of which there are five:

Eastern Operations: responsible for a geographic spread of field based offices. Eastern is the largest Operating Unit representing some 30% of the firm's total income.

Western Operations: responsible for a geographic spread of field based offices. A smaller Operating Unit representing some 15% of the firm's income, however very fast growing and seen to be innovative.

Southern Operations: responsible for a geographic spread of field based offices and representing some 25% of the firm's income.

Central Support: provides specialised expertise to the other Units, plus deals with a small number of nationwide clients who account for 20% of income.

International Business: responsible for all non-US business, mostly in Western Europe. Not seen as strategic but quite profitable and accounting for 10% of income.

Charlie is currently trying to co-ordinate the purchase of a new customer records and billing system, and has decided to ask the three current incumbents to bid:

TotalMan (you) have an old V1 system covering 50% of Eastern Operations offices and 30% of Southern Operations offices; you also have a V2 System used by 30% of the International offices and a brand new V3 System covering all of the Western Operation offices.

Proproff have 50% of Eastern offices and 20% of Southern offices.

Matterhorn Systems have 50% of Southern, 100% of Central and 70% of International offices.

None of the above systems are compatible, although the various versions of the TotalMan system can communicate well with each other. The Proproff system could be upgraded quite easily to be compatible with your systems. The Matterhorn system is completely non-compatible however is capable of basic data exchange with TotalMan V3 systems.

Following a discussion with your Competitive Watch Team, you made the following notes:

TotalMan V1
- Strengths: does a good job
- Weaknesses: limited functionality

TotalMan V2
- Strengths: industry standard; lots of add-on features available
- Weaknesses: limited functionality in base system

TotalMan V3
- Strengths: Broad feature set and good pricing
- Weaknesses: OK but not great with international features

Proproff
- Strengths: Flexible, cheap, easy to deploy
- Weaknesses: Lacking some features

Matterhorn
- Strengths: Feature rich, international presence
- Weaknesses: Proprietary, not very flexible, expensive

Two hugely complicating issues are that the CIO's in each Business Unit have slightly different agendas and the funding is coming partly from Charlie Walker's central budget and partly from the Business Unit own funds:

Sanjiv Mehra is the CIO for Eastern Operations and is due to retire in two years time. He has stated that a 'stable platform' is his number one priority, and while you have a good relationship with him you are aware that he can be quite easily swayed by colleagues. Eastern have committed to at least match whatever central funding is provided.

In Western Operations you have your strongest Supporter, Janice O'Regan who is a formidable lady being aggressive and ambitious and who is looking to create a showcase environment. Western Operations have committed to match and then add on another 50% to whatever central funding is made available. In addition, Janice has told you that she wants you to ensure that her system is the most advanced of all and with the highest capability.

She has also already told you in confidence that her plan is to offer a managed service to the rest of Rucker & Willems, and longer-term she wants Western Operations to effectively supply the company wide ICT organisation.

Ron Princeton is the CIO for Southern Operations. Ron is known as a bit of a maverick, and likes to do his own thing and you know that he has a preference for Proproff. Southern are struggling financially at the moment and have said that they want to spend as little as possible on this system – in fact they believe that central funding alone should enable them to upgrade their current system to make it compatible with whatever is the corporate standard.

In Central Support John Esterhaus is acting CIO and it is unclear whether or not he will get the job permanently. While you have a good relationship with John, he is very technical and can be quite stubborn. He will be swayed by the technical elegance of a solution and is very tied to a Matterhorn proposal. Central Support have said that they will match the funding from Charlie Walker, and you think that John will try to find money from elsewhere if necessary to keep his current supplier.

You know very little about Jean-Claude Folliet the CIO for International. Publically he has stated that flexibility is of paramount importance, although you are uncertain about his real desires and agenda. You do know that International are likely to match central funding.

Things have suddenly accelerated as Charlie has been told that CAPEX budget has suddenly become available, provided that it is committed, with a firm PO sent out, by the end of the quarter in five weeks time.

Charlie has requested a meeting in the next 48 hours, and wants to know:

- Are you intending to put in five bids for each of the divisions
- Might you also put in a single bid to cover everything
- Will you give the same level of discount to each of the five Business Units.

You need to decide how to answer Charlie, and also what your overall strategy will be for this great opportunity.

Real Account Planning

What would you do? There are no 'right' or 'wrong' answers to Case Examples such as this, which are designed to help in thinking through classic situations, which sometimes get clouded when you have the myriad amounts of data in a real life account. You can go to www.realaccountplanning.com/Cases to read a selection of model responses and also to make your own comments.

Classic Strategy Questions: Central or Divisional

Every account situation will reveal new strategic choices to be decided upon, but one very common classical question is whether or not to focus and align with one centralised function or multiple business units that may be spread throughout the organisation:

In many organisations strategy and decision-making are a combination of centralised functions and divisional / business unit / geographically distributed functions. For example IT strategy and architecture is often the responsibility of the corporate ICT function, but individual buying decisions may be left to individual units.

The dilemma for real Account Managers is that the central functions and the individual business units are often in conflict. Central functions will want to impose corporate wide standards and common processes, whereas business units will want solutions that meet their precise business needs. Of course, behind these kind of issues is a pure power play, with central functions needing and wanting to exert their control over the operating units (otherwise why do they exist) and operating units attempting to gain greater and greater autonomy.

While these issues are playing out technically there are probably similar issues with central procurement groups having more or less control over their local equivalents, as well as finance and operations groups wanting to preserve and build their own powerbases.

Real Account Planning

Into this maelstrom of technical issues, politics and power plays, the real Account Manager must tread very carefully. Most Account Mangers want to be aware of but not play a part in the politics of an account, and while this is understandable, in many cases it is simply not possible.

Real Account Managers weigh up where power currently sits, and more importantly how it is shifting, as most organisations go through constant centralise / decentralise phases every few years. Then they will weigh up which options are available to them and which will yield greatest long term success, while giving acceptable short term results (in most sales organisations you can make some long term relationship investments, but there will always be pressure for some short term returns).

Classic available options include:

Firm Centralised Alignment: could be the optimal strategy if you are perceived as a strong incumbent and the central function has high levels of power (but this needs checking out as central functions are rarely as powerful as they will tell you).

Guerrilla Warfare: is where you have a poor or no relationship centrally and fight each battle individually in the operating units, with no reference back to the central function. Ideally each individual project will be 'under the radar' of the central function and this could well be a good initial strategy, but will probably need to be developed over time.

Surround and Strangle: useful where solutions are technically somehow interdependent, for example co-operating user application software. Possibly an extension of Guerrilla Warfare but accepting that the central function may become aware. Centrally they may try to erect technical, political or procurement barriers, but will eventually have to go along with pressure from individual users or operating companies.

Double Agents: A very difficult strategy to execute, reliant on having different individuals working with the operating companies and with the centralised functions. One variation open to suppliers who work with Business Partners (resellers or integrators) is to use different organisations in different units, with the Account Manager coordinating, probably behind the scenes. All kinds of issues can arise from this approach, however it often fits in with the reality of historical business development by the vendor and their independent Business Partners.

In reality most account strategies in large complex accounts will involve a variation of these types of approaches, depending on the history, current positioning and future potential. The real Account Manager however will carefully balance the options available and make conscious choices around this central question, and not just let it drift or be dictated by the customer.

Classic Strategy Questions: Technical or Business or Procurement

In managing the relationship with any account there are often three big constituents that have to be considered: Technical, Procurement and Business.

The Technical function for your products and services will look for technical excellence in your offering, probably with a strong regard for standards, compatibility and interoperability with other systems, including legacy systems.

The Business functions have the need for your products and services and will probably be driving requirements and the business case.

The Procurement function will vary in power depending on the politics of the account, but will normally want to ensure fair process according to the metrics that have been put in place, for example 'best value' or 'supplier stability'.

Procurement functions will often be judged against their own metrics, which may not be fully aligned with the business functions. For example typically business functions will evaluate options based on impact on the bottom line business results such as EBITDA. Procurement on the other hand may be solely judged (and remunerated) on top line savings or in some cases the level of price reductions that can be obtained from suppliers.

All real Account Managers will have learned very early in their career that you cannot treat the account as one customer – it is a collection of individuals and dynamic groupings who all need to be treated differently.

As with all aspects of proactive real Account Planning the real Account Manager will consciously evaluate how to interact with the various constituents, including who in the Account Team leads particular aspects of the relationship.

For example many Account Teams will include a Technical Account Manager, normally from the Pre-Sales function, who will drive particular relationships and may even produce a separate Technical Account Plan (hopefully a real Plan!). In a similar fashion if there is on-going support for operational systems, a separate Service Delivery or Client Operations Manager will be a key part of the Account Team, developing the appropriate relationships as part of the overall Account Plan.

Classic Strategy Questions: Full-Frontal or Flanking

Full-Frontal and Flanking are classic strategies for Single Sales Opportunities, which can also be applied to account development.

A Full-Frontal Strategy is based on taking the customer's initial stated requirements and evaluation criteria, then relating your offering with its strengths and benefits against these stated requirements.

A Flanking Strategy (also called a Basis Change Strategy) seeks to change the customer stated requirements and / or evaluation criteria. How you go about this will generally involve a combination of two approaches. A Consultative (often referred to as Solution or Value-based) selling approach with key stakeholders will seek to take them back to the business or operational issues that they are facing, and from that point work forward to the solution requirements, obviously along the way stressing those aspects where you will have a superiority. At the same time a skilful working of the relationships in the Playing Field will attempt to get issues, requirements and evaluation criteria favourable to your cause raised by your Supporters or others who would gain from aligning against these issues.

A variation of the Flanking Strategy is a Segmentation approach where you seek to package or frame the overall requirement into a series of discrete solutions, some of which you can pick off through your superiority in these areas.

As well as breaking up an overall solution with a Segmentation approach, sometimes a Consolidation Strategy will be more favourable to you, where you attempt to combine initially separate requests into one whole; obviously this is a useful approach where you have massive strength in one area that can leverage business in other areas where you are less strong.

The art of strategy in all but the Full Frontal Strategy is to make sure that you are picking battle grounds that are favourable to you. This is true at the start of particular sales opportunities, and even more appropriate in real Account Development where you will be planning, preparing and positioning for future battles well in advance of them becoming recognised buying projects.

Classic Strategy Questions: All or Partial

The Segmentation Strategy described above and relevant to an approach to individual Opportunities can also be applied to long term account strategy.

In the vast majority of cases our relationship with a customer will start with an initial engagement, normally a specific solution within a specific part of the organisation.

To win an initial engagement it will more often than not be that the proposition and messaging was around how specialised your organisation is in providing this solution that is perfectly tuned to the real business and / or technical requirements of the customer. It is rare that a customer chooses a new supplier on the basis of knowing them well and having deep trust in them to satisfy a multitude of requirements.

But having won the initial toe-hold into the account, unless you are a single product company, then you will want to expand your presence into new solutions, new operating areas and new geographies.

The dilemma facing all Account Managers in this situation though is that the positioning that gave you initial success (a specialist in a particular area and ideally suited to the initial application in the specific business area and / or geography) is now at odds with how you may want to be positioned as a broad supplier and trusted partner in a multitude of areas.

In addition to overall positioning in the minds of the customer is the issue of relationships. Your existing contacts may not be comfortable with you talking to others around the organisation, for a number of reasons including not wishing their business dealings to be exposed, not trusting you to paint them in the best possible light, not wishing to have the relationship diluted etc.

For these reasons the issue of how far and how quickly to expand outside of your initial base within the account is often difficult for Account Managers.

The factors that they would often consider when deciding on how aggressively to pursue any growth goals will include:

- Estimate of what other potential could be worth

- How much of a risk might there be to current relationships and business levels

- Views of their existing contacts

- State of the competition in the account, both generally and in any particular target areas

- Being certain about how you are perceived and in particular how much you are trusted

- Ease of getting to other potential worthwhile contacts

- Ability to use others to penetrate into other areas of the account; for example use of overlay sales specialists or Business Partners

As with most military campaigns, the questions to ask are: Is it potentially worth it? Will it leave my current position exposed? Is it doable?

Classic Strategy Questions: One-off or On-going and Stickiness

When reviewing Account Plans it is amazing the number that are fixated on one decision, normally a short or medium term project. There are sometimes good reasons for this, such as:

- Especially in smaller customers, they may only buy one major project every few years; this may be true if, for example, you are selling a phone system or a CRM system to a Small and Medium Enterprise account

- On occasions, a single purchase decision may set the scene for future business; the opportunity may be seen as a pilot, or the politics suggest that this one decision will set a precedent which will be very hard to overturn

- The project may be so large that due to its orders / revenue potential it requires particular focus

On the other hand, there are reasons why just focusing on the next big project will be detrimental to business:

- Winning a pilot is good, but will be expensive and only worth it if you have a clear plan to make sure that you then capture on-going business; there are many examples where a supplier has been happy for a competitor to trail-blaze and go through the hard work of proving a concept, and then to come in with a reduced price or a killer feature when the major roll-out appears

- By just focusing on the immediate project, you will fail to set the foundations for future business; many deals are effectively won or lost in the period before they are recognised as a qualified project

- Without a clear view of where you are heading, you will transmit to the customer that you are only interested in short term grabbing of business

- You may win the deal but leave yourself weak to develop further business due to your positioning (overall proposition and messaging) being too specialised, or your political mapping being too narrow. It is not uncommon for all your resources to be focused on say a departmental win, and you are then locked-in to relationships at this level and this part of the overall organisation

Clearly, in the vast majority of cases, when there is a major project opportunity available in the near term, then this will deserve a strong focus, however this should be put into the context of a long term plan. You need to see how you are going to win the overall war, as well as all of the major battles along the way.

Allied to this is the whole concept of 'stickiness', which in our context, is normally defined as the likelihood that an account will continue buying from you.

Increasing stickiness is often a key aim of a real Account Plan as it will lead to more business, at a lower cost of sale, with higher levels of predictability. When focusing on a major project, the on-going stickiness of your relationship should be a big consideration. There are many elements that can affect overall stickiness including:

- **Contractual:** clearly if your account is totally locked into buying a certain class of products or services from you, then stickiness can be almost guaranteed for the period of the contract (but beware overstepping here, as customers will try to find ways to break contracts that are not in their best interests, and will certainly seek vengeance once they can get out of a contract that they perceived as unfair)

- **Financial:** pricing and rebates can be used to encourage customers to keep coming back to you (and often clever and creative models can be developed)

- **Technical:** on occasions a technical strategy can be developed which lock people into to a certain architecture and then a limited number of products and services that can fit into that architecture. Even if you do not have full lock-in, then the technical strategy should at least give you advantage in terms of compatibility etc.

- **Physical Security:** as a key lever can be used to increase stickiness. Often related to a technical strategy, security is about ensuring through compatibility that upgrades, additions, revisions and changes can occur without risk to the customer

- **Emotional Security:** in many cases while physical security is important, it is the perceived uncertainty or risk that plays a bigger part in ensuring stickiness. Even if physical security cannot be 100% guaranteed, there is a very strong argument that retaining existing suppliers will lead to a reduced effective risk, particularly if the supplier can reference a long history of going beyond the strict contractual limits to ensure smooth operations (better the devil that you know, particularly if that devil has got you out of difficult situations in the past)

- **Operational:** ease of operational use is a good motivator for the technical people responsible day to day for your solution to want to continue to do business with you. Many real Account Managers include operational and service or support elements in their plans. For example regular review meetings where all aspects of the solution can be reviewed and any issues fixed, is a good way of making life easier for the Operational people involved (and can provide added intelligence as to what is happening in the account)

- **Presence in their world:** for both sound business, technical, operational and emotional reasons people want to buy services and products that are common in their own world. An easy example is the spread of Apps, especially those that communicate with each other, but the power of familiarity is also a strong reason why people will continue to buy from a particular supplier

- **Political:** buying decisions are very often political decisions, and ensuring that the politics continue to favour your position is key to success for a real Account Manager. Aligning yourself and the team with key individuals involved or affecting the buying decisions will often mean that those in your favour will simply get passed so much easier, and conversely any individual in the customer who wants to try and push through competitive vendors knows that they will have a difficult time, leading them to often choose not to fight that battle

- **Administrative:** because certain buying decisions are often made tactically and in short time, managing the administration of doing business with your organisation can sometimes be key. Just as much of politics is about 'responding to events' so a good real Account Manager will prepare through the Account Plan for any events that will occur, such as a sudden release of money that has to be spent, an unexpected business event such as the acquisition of new people or buildings etc. Taking the time to invest in making sure that the people who have to physically go through the buying process find dealing with you easy and without risk, will often make a significant difference when things get decided quickly and without thorough evaluation

- ***Channel / partners:*** the influence of 'channel' partners (both upstream vendors and downstream resellers) can often be overlooked in the Account Plan; this has many implications, one of which is the amount of stickiness of your offerings

- ***Emotional:*** the emotional bonds between individuals (and sometimes with an organisation) can be incredibly strong. The years of taking people to sports events, having lunch, discussing their family life, getting them out of holes that they have dug for themselves – all these things are important and will come into play when you are trying to influence and shape emerging projects and when future buying decisions are made

Summary

- *Points of Entry, Points of Power and Points of Pain can be used to help navigate around the Account, and as a concept to help with the relationship strategy when trying to develop demand for new solutions within an Account*

- *Developing Value is about relating the real benefits of your solution to the business and personal issues of the people involved, and being rigorous in quantifying the full value that can be gained*

- *Solution Development can start with Solution Mapping, a form of reverse engineering the value proposition*

- *Progressive Selling recognises that good qualified Opportunities only come about from Possibilities, where people have been considering a particular course of action. Possibilities are generated by relationships and conversations*

- *Player Mapping is a standard technique for ensuring that over time you have good and full coverage of all the individuals that you might want to have relationships with*

- *Exec Sponsorship is often discussed yet rarely implemented properly, when it can be incredibly powerful in the account development and selling effort*

- *All good real Account Managers appear to have a knack for, and put a lot of effort into spotting, developing and nurturing their Agents (Supporters)*

- *It is worthwhile to consider the Classic Strategy questions:*
  - *Central vs. Divisional*
  - *Technical / Business / Procurement focus*
  - *Full-Frontal or Flanking*
  - *All or Partial*
  - *One-off vs. On-going and Stickiness*

Real Account Planning

PART 4: IMPLEMENTING REAL ACCOUNT PLANNING

"The best way to predict the future is to invent it."

Alan Kay, Apple Fellow

"Vision without execution is just pure hallucination"

Henry Ford

Plans and the Planning Process

We have already seen that it is vitally important to have high quality, succinct plans in place which accurately describe the current situation with your account, and set out meaningful Goals, Objectives, Strategies and Tactics. This will enable the real Account Manager, the whole Account Team, sales management and others to effectively manage the customer business relationship and derive maximum value from each significant customer.

Sometimes we forget however that the plan itself is in some ways of secondary importance – the primary benefit is often in the process that we go through.

Taking time out as an Account Manager, or preferably the core Account Team, standing back from the intense pressure of day-to-day activities and figuring out exactly what the current relationship is with your customer, brainstorming opportunities, reviewing different strategies and making conscious decisions about what you will do in the future with this customer; these activities are what brings the whole topic alive and are the real benefit of having a robust Account Planning Programme in place.

When embarking upon Account Planning most organisations, and most sales leaders focus on the template that is to be completed. Intense debate can be had about exact wordings of sections and how to integrate with existing CRM or Salesforce Automation systems.

The format that you decide upon for your Account Plan template is important, and in a following section there are some observations from practical experience and a few firm recommendations. However please don't fall into the trap of believing that having designed the 'form' you are ready to implement an effective Account Planning programme. This applies to senior Sales Leadership, Sales Ops people and individual Account Managers.

The best organisations, those where Account Planning actually works (demonstrably driving higher levels of revenue and profit over time) spend much more time in developing the process of Account Planning.

Segmentation of Accounts

Most organisations will segment their account base in some way to allow for sensible management of portfolios and to provide focus on where to apply sales and marketing resources.

A real Account Manager with a manageable number of accounts will also normally segment their own portfolio, allowing him or her the ability to focus in different ways on different customers, and helping to decide which accounts would benefit from a full real Account Development Plan.

A very simple tool from ProAct Business Development is typical of a pragmatic approach to account segmentation. The four box segmentation looks at a customer's current and recent Performance, which is normally very easily measured by orders or revenues. The model then considers account Potential, which will be more of a judgment, based on how much growth you can envisage. The factors that you might take into account when looking at growth potential would include:

- The account business performance (are they expanding / contracting)

- Their appetite for change (which will lead to new requirements) and often heavily influenced by what is happening in their industry

- How many of your solutions are they currently buying?

- Your wallet share versus competitors

By looking at these two key factors, we can quickly determine four broad types of accounts from an Account Management perspective:

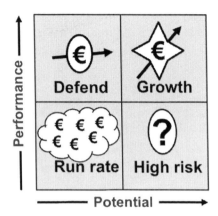

High Risk Accounts are new, break-in types of accounts, where to be successful you are going to have to commit a lot of energy and resources, with a high risk that you will not be successful. With High Risk accounts your strategy will be one of continual qualification and either gaining a presence before growing the business (a land and expand strategy) or going for a very high risk Knockout Strategy.

Growth Accounts are those accounts that are yielding good business today and also have long term potential to deliver even more. These accounts should have a robust, well considered real Account Plan with measured use of resources. These are excellent accounts to have in the portfolio, and should be given priority whenever appropriate.

Defend Accounts will have given us good business in the past, but have either plateaued or are 'one-hit wonders'. Their business may be in decline or they are saturated in terms of how much business they could do with us. From a resourcing perspective, Defend Accounts are the ones that should give the most concern.

It is very easy to become complacent about these accounts and not give them the attention that they deserve, which will only serve to hasten their demise.

On the other hand, it is very easy to over resource these accounts, the more so if they are very large and have been doing business with you for some time. They probably know all of the routes into your business and who to call to get resources. They can make contact directly with technical or support people, and can easily escalate issues to senior management, who they may have met numerous times over the years. They end up sucking resources out of you, often in the name of 'customer satisfaction'.

The strategy with Defend Accounts should be one of giving them enough attention and resources to keep them reasonably happy and continuing with current business levels, but not too much resource that you end up not having enough to invest in High Risk or Growth Accounts.

Run Rate Accounts are not particularly exciting today, and in your judgment will not be exciting in the near future.

They should not be ignored, because taken together the business levels may be quite reasonable, and as situations change, future Growth opportunities could emerge from this pool of accounts.

In most cases, the strategy with Run Rate Accounts is to treat them as a programme. Make sure that they receive regular contact, but in a low-cost way (newsletters, seminar invitations etc.) and schedule visits to them on a regular but infrequent basis, making sure that time is used efficiently, for example coinciding with visits to nearby other accounts.

This is a very simple Account Segmentation model, and there are others that are more sophisticated to deal with national and multi-national accounts, exploring not just total performance but looking at 'strategic' products or services that you may want to focus on.

In practice real Account Managers always adopt some form of segmentation. Spending an hour or so as an individual, or as part of a team, with post it notes or cards and examining the complete portfolio of accounts, is time very well spent.

Having arrived at the segmentation, this will form the basis of deciding which accounts to start the account planning process with and where to focus efforts.

The challenge then is to make sure that you keep the segmentation in mind during all of your dealings, prioritising resources into High Risk and Growth Accounts, giving appropriate attention to Defend Accounts (not allowing them to suck you in or taking them for granted) and disciplining yourself to keep some form of efficient communication with Run Rate Accounts.

The Template

As has been stressed a number of times, the actual template does not appear in practice to be the most critical element in real Account Planning. There are many templates available which can be perfect in some cases but useless in other cases because the whole programme and process have not been implemented correctly.

For most organisations, while the template should not be important, it is good to have a level of commonality that makes generating and using high quality plans easy for everyone concerned. A good template will have a number of characteristics:

- Primary design point is the Account Manager and the core Account Team; encouraging and supporting them to produce real Account Plans which develop increased business over time

- Others who need access to Account Plans and the information contained are the secondary audience

- Consistent yet flexible – in reality different accounts will justify different levels of detail and different perspectives

- Easy to use and easy to update

- Where possible integrated with any sales force automation system (in particular action plans) so as to make implementation efficient and effective; however this should not be the primary consideration.

- Can be stored and shared with adequate ease of access and security controls

- Can be modified easily to suit different purposes, for example presenting an outline to the wider Account Team, sharing with Business Partners, sharing with the end customer etc.

We have resisted the temptation to be prescriptive about the template for a good real Account Plan, because having ownership of the whole process is crucial, and the actual template should be tuned to the particular situation and needs of each selling team, however some examples from ProAct Business Development and elsewhere are included in the appendices.

Plan Hierarchy

Real Account Planning is not a one-off activity but part of a structured way of going about the whole selling business. A good real Account manager will be constantly planning and will view the real Account Plan as one key tool in a hierarchy:

Overall Business Plan
Account Portfolio / Territory Plan
Account Plans
Opportunity Plans
Call Plans

All of these plans can be either formal or informal, and SA-GOST is a good overall format for all of them.

Acquisition Accounts

During Account Review sessions we often have to answer the question: is this whole process applicable to New or Acquisition accounts? A short discussion will generally clarify this point and lead to the conclusion that real Account Plans are absolutely relevant for new accounts, with the following provisos:

- Completing a good Situation Analysis is as relevant for new account acquisition as it is for on-going Account Management and Development, however you will probably be amazed at the amount of information that you do not know and some early actions will involve simple information gathering

- You will be taking actions anyway, so it will be better to have thought these through earlier on (and this is just what real Account Planning is all about!)

- You may well have some very short term Milestones which are in effect go / no go points where you need to decide on whether or not to pursue opportunities in this organisation

- Strategies will often be slanted very much around developing relationships especially getting beyond initial Points of Entry to Points of Pain and then starting to create demand through the value of your particular offerings (see Part 3 for further discussion on these topics)

For Sales Leadership

By the Process of Account Planning we mean have sales leadership thought through and decided upon issues such as:

- Which accounts deserve full account planning being applied to them?

- Who is involved in developing the Plan?

- Who reviews the plan over what timescales?

- Do you store all plans together centrally, if so how do you ensure security of information, especially if you have a multi-channel organisation where effectively Channel Account Managers may be competing for the same business?

- Do you integrate the Account Plan documentation with your CRM / SFA system?

- As well as reviewing plans, do you have a formal sign-off process?

- What is the primary purpose of an account review; is it information sharing, coaching, decision making, formal sign-off, supporting (see the section on reviewing account plans later)?

- How do you integrate with any other customer facing plans, for example Service Delivery Plans, Vertical Industry Marketing Plans?

- How do you handle National and International accounts with potentially multiple Account Managers?

- How do you integrate with event or Opportunity based plans, for example Bid Reviews?

- How do you gain the support and buy-in of all the business, including other functional managers?

The Comovian case study that follows presents some typical answers to these questions, with a rationale, however in all cases it is for senior sales leadership to design the process appropriate to your environment and in the context of what you are trying to achieve with Account Plans.

As with the design of the actual Plan Template, good experienced consultants can be a great help, inputting not only their experience of having implemented many programmes, but also providing an independent perspective. However one of the factors that appears critical in any implementation is that field Sales Management need to own the whole process. Similarly if there is a Sales Operations function then they will need to be heavily involved in the detailed implementation and to ensure smooth running of systems and processes, however sponsorship needs to rest firmly with senior sales leadership.

For Account Managers

While your organisation will provide you with the framework for developing Account Plans, you will still have some choices to make, and depending on how Account Planning is being implemented, these will include:

- Are you really going to treat this seriously, or simply pay lip service to the company process? (we have strong views on this, which are hopefully apparent, and the fact that you have read this far indicates that you will make the right choice here!)

- Which accounts do you want to develop plans for, and at what depth?

- While you have to accept that as the Account Manager you are ultimately responsible for the Account Plan, you will have to decide who else to involve in the initial creation, in refining and in reviewing the plan

- How often do you and the Account Team come together to review and refine the Plan; at what point do you invest time in a complete re-write of the Plan?

- Joint Planning has its own chapter in this book, however without formal Joint Planning, do you want to involve the customer in any way in the planning process?

- What about Business Partners; both other organisations that you re-sell through as well as others who have an interest that at least partially intersects with your own such as consultants and suppliers of complementary products or services?

- How often and in what ways do you want to involve sales management in the process?

For Sales Leadership: Comovian Case Study

Comovian are a provider of communications equipment, working mostly with partners to provide complete solutions to SME and Enterprise customers globally.

Their sales strategy involves using High Touch Account Managers to develop business with their top accounts although they will predominantly supply through a Business Partner. In the SME space they are wholly reliant on Business Partners and rarely make direct contact with the end-user.

Justine Bayer, SVP of Global Sales has identified Account Planning as a key opportunity area for the corporation after her Sales Operations Manager had conducted an analysis of selling costs, levels of repeat and leveraged business (cross selling new product streams into existing customers). In some regions around the world Account Planning had been championed by local management and they had done a far better job in both lowering overall selling costs and in cross selling.

Bayer's first task was to ask one of her up and coming Regional VP's to lead a global effort to determine existing best practice inside Comovian and in the industry. A series of meetings and briefings then followed after which she approved the following guidelines:

- Account Planning to be initiated across all regions, based on a standard 8-slide template

- Regions can vary the format where it makes sense, although 5 of the 8 slides she considered mandatory

- Account Planning to be a separate exercise from transactional business and Plans should NOT be held in Salesforce.com which is the Comovian corporate standard

This last point generated lot of healthy debate however in the end Bayer decided that the activity of standing back from the day to day tactical business needed a separate focus; she did agree that the resultant tactical Action Plans should be stored in Salesforce.

- Account Managers are responsible for the Account Plan, but as a minimum should involve a Core Account Team including Pre-Sales Technical Account Manager and Service Account

Manager; In addition they would be encouraged to involve others in the creation of the Plan and to share the Plan with everyone who touched the account in any way

- All Account Mangers to have Account Plans for at least their Top 3 Accounts (end users and / or Business Partners) in place by the end of the year and formally reviewed at least every six months
- Account Plans to be available on demand to senior management, and a new field in Salesforce.com used to indicate when the Plan was last updated and reviewed
- The Selling Excellence Group within Global Sales to have a roving remit to look at the quality of Account Plans and to share best practice
- The Western Division to run a series of facilitated Joint Planning workshops with key Business Partners to develop both overall Joint Sales and Marketing Plans, and also Joint Plans for some carefully targeted end user accounts. If successful in generating incremental business, these to be rolled out across the whole sales organisation

To get the ball rolling she mandated that each of her direct reports should present the Top Three Plans under their remit during an upcoming sales leadership team meeting (and she insisted that they had to do it personally) and could invite Account Managers to attend, but only to answer any detailed questions; she also heavily encouraged her direct reports to do the same for all of their reports.

For Account Managers: Comovian Case Study

Comovian are a provider of communications equipment, working mostly with Business Partners to provide complete solutions to SME and Enterprise customers globally.

Their sales strategy involves using High Touch Account Managers to develop business with their top accounts although they will predominantly supply through a Business Partner.

Michael Solaffson is an Account Manager responsible for fifteen accounts in total of which four would be regarded as major accounts; they are doing significant business today and have great potential to do more in the future through a combination of their own internal growth and their ability to consume more Comovian offerings.

Michael is an experienced Account Manager with a number of year's success behind him. During his career he has been involved in various Account Planning initiatives with different companies and different managers, and while he believes in the concept he has never really achieved a Plan that is a 'living, breathing document guiding our actions'. His experience is that most sales managers insist on Account Plans for a short period, but then rarely follow up and use the investment of time wisely.

Initially Michael was very sceptical of this latest initiative from Comovian corporate, but he respected Justine Bayer, SVP of Global Sales and also believes that Account Plans could be really good tools, as long as they don't become bureaucratic processes that never get followed up.

He was pleasantly surprised that he only had to complete a few slides and only on his top three accounts by end of the year, although having considered this for a while he personally decided to produce Plans for his top four accounts over the next four months.

The slide deck that he had been given was fine and allowed him to focus on the key issues that could really accelerate growth in his accounts.

In considering who to involve in the Account Planning process Michael sought some advice from the corporate Selling Excellence Group and decided that for Holland & Green his most significant account he would put together a task team of himself, a Solution Architect who is currently engaged with the customer, the Technical Account Manager, the assigned Inside Sales

Representative and the Service Delivery Manager. The advice had been that five people was the maximum that would normally be involved in creating the first draft, and this group had a good blend of experience, knowledge of the account and also different outlooks on business.

For his other accounts Michael was planning just to involve the TAM and SDM, although for all four he was drawing up a list of the Extended Account Team, who would be circulated on the first draft and asked for their comments. He subsequently decided that for SolusCor, his second largest account, that he would involve the Account Manager from Manterno, his channel Business Partner, who have always worked exclusively with Comovian on this particular customer, and where Michael has already built a good relationship.

Having discussed his accounts briefly with the Selling Excellence Group, Michael decided to use different approaches to developing the Plans for his four different accounts:

Holland & Green: he would ask his Inside Sales Rep to do most of the background information gathering (Situation Analysis) and then spend two half days with the core Account Team brainstorming possibilities and deciding on actions

SolusCor: as he had a very good knowledge of this very stable customer, Michael decided to write a draft plan himself, and then ask the Core Team to review it with a view to making significant improvements

City of Redpool: another stable account where Comovian are well entrenched as the primary supplier, with a very long-term contract but with some opportunity for upgrades and additions. Michael decided to ask the Service Delivery Manager to lead the Account Planning process, with a brief to focus on maximising revenues and customer satisfaction, but also making the whole customer facing operation as efficient and effective as possible

Shoretons: this is a new account where Comovian have won an initial implementation but where there is huge potential. Michael decided that he could document the Situation Analysis, but then ask the Core Account Team to get together and be as creative as possible in suggesting new possible approaches and different angles from which to exploit the account potential. With this in mind he decided to invite one of the local Marketing Managers to the event, someone who is well known for often having zany ideas

Michael did not consider that his relationship with any of his accounts was sufficiently strong to do a proper Joint Planning exercise, although he resolved to share at least part of the Situation Analysis and some of his Strategies with his main contact at two of his customers. He also set himself a personal objective of getting his relationships sufficiently strong, in at least one account, so that he could carry out a facilitated Joint Planning session within twelve months.

Challenging your own real Account Plans

Having reviewed literally thousands of account plans, it is obvious that in over half of cases, the Account Team simply challenging themselves more rigorously could significantly improve the plan.

As an Account Manager or an Account Team, having taken the trouble to put a good plan together, a little more investment of time and energy in refining it, through a process of challenge, can give dramatic results. There are many methods that you can adopt, with one of the most simple and most effective being as follows:

- Make sure that the plan in draft form is complete in terms of content (don't worry with cosmetics at this stage, because the content is going to change)

- Put yourself in the position of someone who is going to review your plan, and list down the questions that they would have and the areas that they will probably want to explore and challenge. You might want to use the 'Ten Tests' that follow, or the example list in the next section of this book. It is normally recommended that this list is compiled each time you complete a plan as all accounts operate in a different context

- Ask the questions and make the challenges to the whole plan, and at each stage write down the response and also how you believe a reviewer might react to the responses; would they be satisfied, impressed, disappointed, unbelieving... and why would they have these reactions?

- Summarise the review by imagining what you believe the reviewer would say when their boss asked them "What did you think of that Account Plan that you reviewed today?"

Ten Tests for your Account Strategy

Inspired by 'Have you tested your strategy lately?' from Chris Bradle, Martin Hirt and Sven Smit which was the most downloaded article from McKinsey Quarterly in 2011, here are the Top 10 Tests that any real Account Manager or real Account Director can apply to their Account Development Plan.

Test 1: Will your strategy beat any incumbent and the market leader?

While it is not bad practice to focus on strong competitors that are appearing at any precise moment and in current particular deals, in practice it is difficult to gain accurate up to date information and benchmark yourself against all possible rivals. Testing your plans against the market leader and any incumbent is often more realistic and effective.

Particularly once you get to the end-game of large deals and once technical recommendations have been made, the market leader and the incumbent will gain increased advantage with senior and more business-oriented decision makers. The market leader is naturally attractive to senior decision makers as they can provide a benchmark against any technical recommendations, while the current incumbent is likely to have relationships to exploit and will often be perceived as the 'low risk' option.

Test 2: Is your strategy granular about where to compete?

Does it address everyone in the Playing Field with individual compelling differentiated Value Propositions, including Financial / Technical / Business people and issues?

Organisations do not make decisions; groups of individuals make decisions. From the analysis of thousands of Account Plans both at initial draft form and during end of year reviews it is clear that success comes to those who are clear about individual compelling value propositions rather than talking about generic 'business challenges'.

The term Playing Field is used to describe the various individuals who will affect decisions, from minor influencers and recommenders to chief decision makers, ratifiers and approvers. A good analysis includes their personal challenges and drivers, decision biases, political importance, allegiance to ourselves and the type of access that we have to them.

Too often Account Managers underestimate the number of people involved and focus too heavily on their immediate (probably mid level technical or procurement based) contacts. In reality in the majority of cases there will be financially oriented and business oriented individuals who will have a significant role in the decision making process, particularly during the end game of a project.

A great strategy will have an overarching organisational Compelling Value Proposition or set of Win Themes, but will then drill down to the individual level, being clear about the proposition to each of the Key Players.

Test 3: Does your strategy take account of the whole channel network of vendors, integrators, consultants and other influencers?

For some suppliers the 'channel strategy' is well understood especially if working through resellers, integrators or prime contractors and in these cases how to handle the various official 'partners' involved or potentially involved will be a key component of the real Account Development Plan.

For the vast majority of suppliers however the full 'ecosystem' of Business Partners as well as consultants, outsourcers, trade bodies and complementary suppliers is often completely ignored or under-valued.

The key discovery when reviewing Account Development Plans is to look at life from the perspectives of different people in the account, and what external influencers affect them. Then to look at those external influencers and what life looks like for them; only by working back and asking 'What is my agenda and who are my influencers?' can you normally gain a full insight into what is happening during buying processes and hence your ability to control and influence that process.

Test 4: Does your strategy address real Business and Operational Imperatives and include a demonstrable Business Case (including ROI) for your solutions?

Individuals and organisations will only buy new complex solutions when there is a compelling Business Case that includes a Return On Investment (ROI) case that is superior to others, and which allows senior management to understand and manage the risks inherent in doing anything new.

Business Cases are becoming increasingly important, and while only the customer can produce a final plausible case, suppliers can help by suggesting areas of savings, phasing of cost / revenue flows, examples of what others have done, running pilots or proof of concept trials for example.

The key to a strong Business Case is often in defining and discovering the full extent of the Operational Imperatives and linking them to Business Imperatives. In the real Account Development Planning process Account Managers use the same approach as in any good consultative selling technique, of concentrating on finding and emphasising customer issues (pains) before addressing any particular solution; we only buy pain-killers when we have a pain, and the more acute we perceive the pain to be, the more likely we are to want to buy a pain-killer!

When working in sales force development it often found that proper real Account Development Planning is closely aligned with instilling a good consultative selling approach.

Test 5: Does your strategy use Full Frontal strategy ONLY where you have overwhelming, demonstrable superiority?

From Sun Tzu through Clausewitz to the vast majority of successful modern marketeers, it is an accepted and obvious truth that to win a head-to-head battle you need overwhelming superiority. Sun Tzu quoted a 3:1 advantage as minimum, whereas others talk about 5:1 or even 10:1.

Yet when reviewing both Account and Opportunity plans, when a Reviewer asks, "Why will they end up buying from you?" the answer that most often comes back is a variation of "Because our widget is a little better than that of the competitors".

By Full Frontal we mean head-to-head battles based on feature / functionality of the particular offering. Even in very straightforward transactional sales of proven products that are well understood by the customer and in a stable market, this approach is fraught with danger and requires very demonstrable superiority. In a fast moving market involving complex offerings bought in a complex, multi-faceted manner, Full Fontal should be the last resort sales strategy. A Flanking / Segmenting type of approach where the point of attack is moved depending on the competitive situation would normally be significantly more effective.

In reality Full Frontal (where overwhelming superiority des not exist) is the strategy most often employed. There are multiple reasons for this including product push from marketing, arriving in complex deals too late and being forced into this approach, lazy sales people or sales people who lack deal understanding and lack of proper training or coaching by sales management.

For a description of Full-Frontal and Flanking Strategies see the Classic Strategy sections of Part 3.

Test 6: Is your strategy supported by and build on significant Internal Support?

It is evident that to be successful in any complex account, inside support (Supporters, inside sales people, Allies, Agents etc.) is vital. They give you the real picture of what is happening, point you in the right direction, open doors for you and can advocate on your behalf when you are not present (the vast majority of the time).

Identifying and understanding the Inside Supporter(s) is critical for success in individual sales opportunities and for longer-term account development. Identifying the individuals is normally fairly straightforward, although many Account Managers make the mistake of believing that just because someone is 'nice' to them, they are automatically a strong Supporter.

Understanding why they support you may be more difficult but gives the real clues as to how to maintain and develop the relationship. Again, reasons for supporting a particular Account Manager or Supplier are often complex and subtle and can include 'better the devil that you know', reduced risks, inherent knowledge of product sets, being different, being one of the herd, not wanting to disappoint someone with whom you have a long relationship, personal liking and family ties!

Understanding the motivations behind support is critical, so that you can develop ways of enhancing and nurturing the support that you will need.

Test 7: Does your strategy embrace uncertainty, balancing commitment and adaptability?

In the military there is a saying that "The plan will change as soon as we get contact with the enemy".

Your real Account Plan will change over time, depending on the changing situation of the customer, technical advances, competitive shifts and changes in the 'Playing Field'.

At the same time, a Plan that is in constant turmoil is hardly a plan at all.

The best Account Plans embrace uncertainty and change, allowing for multiple approaches depending on how situations play out. At the same time they understand what needs to be committed to for the longer term and executed in a disciplined and consistent manner.

Great real Account Managers understand the need for fall-back positions, alternate strategies (often putting in 'gates' to the plan) and the attractiveness of strategies that can be successful under many different conditions. They will schedule account review sessions in advance and constantly challenge themselves to adapt and refine the Plan to ensure that it always represents the best possible chance of success.

Test 8: Is your Plan contaminated by bias?

Sales people are mostly by their nature optimists, seeing the opportunities and positives in most situations. They are generally urged on by sales managers who are constantly pushing for better results, and encouraged by marketeers, business managers, suppliers and business partners all of whom will put a positive spin on their particular areas of business.

So it is little surprise that there is a temptation to contaminate your plan and particularly your strategies by bias, tending to look at the world through your own rose coloured spectacles. This is enormously dangerous as it leads to false understanding during the Situation Analysis phase of planning, as well as unrealistic Goals and Objectives, and Strategies that are only wish lists.

Good real Account Managers understand this and for most the technique that they most often employ to rid themselves of this unhealthy bias it to put themselves 'in the shoes of the customer'. They constantly approach the situation from the perspective of 'Why will this account continue wanting to buy increasing amounts from us?' rather than 'what can we sell them?'

Normally this is a great technique for ensuring that the plan is based in reality. Another very powerful approach can be to get the customer themselves involved in the analysis, creation and refining of the plan. This is discussed more in Part 5 and has to be approached carefully, however it can both ensure reality and build a self-fulfilling prophecy where the customer will be personally motivated to see the plan become successful.

Test 9: Is there conviction by the whole Account Team / Company to act on your strategy with sufficient quality and quantity of resources? Do all of your plans include full bid costs, implementation risks as well as short and longer term risk / reward?

Especially in the New Norm of Selling since 2008, the days of the 'lone-wolf' sales person are firmly over. Buying decisions have become more complex and more scrutinised and while individual relationships with the Account Manager continue to be important, of even more criticality are organisational relationships.

The real Account Plan is a tool for the Account Manager to develop a complete team approach, and also the embodiment of what the organisation will do in terms of this particular customer.

The Account Plan also serves as a process to formulate and agree the internal business case, balancing resources required against potential rewards.

Test 10: Have you translated your strategy into a clear, committed Tactical Action Plan?

There are many examples of really well crafted Account Plans which analyse the customer situation and history in great detail, are very clear about what is desired as objectives, and describe in rich terms the strategies to be adopted.

Many of these plans however fail miserably both as plans and in their execution, because there is no direct action that is committed.

A plan needs a very clear set of tactics or actions that can go straight onto someone's To Do list. Tactics should be clear about what is expected to happen, by when, who is responsible, resources (budget, people etc.) to be used and any outcomes defined.

As it is often said, the Tactical Action Plan is 'where the rubber hits the road'. It provides absolute clarity as to what the next and future steps will be, and without it the Account Manager cannot hope to manage execution of the plan to meet goals.

Some balancing and judgement is required. The best real Account Plans are detailed enough to provide clarity of who is going to do what by when, but at the same time not detailing every phone call or even every meeting, as clearly this could overwhelm the Account Team and also obscure the really important critical actions.

The above section was first published as an article in Winning Edge magazine, the journal of the British Institute of Sales and Marketing Management. The full article, and others, can be downloaded from www.realaccountplanning.com.

Case Example: ShopSys

What Would You Do ?

ShopSys are a successful and growing supplier of retail systems and services, mainly focused on the independent, and more dynamic end of the market. Internally they use technology extensively and see it as a key enabler of their growth and relevance to customers. Historically they have supplied traditional store based systems to their clients, but are now embarking on offering cloud services.

Historically they have tended to regard different technical functions as being quite separate in terms of purchase decisions, with unique approaches to EPOS systems, in-house IT Infrastructure and voice solutions. They also have a large Contact Centre which is used to provide contract telemarketing and telesales services to their clients.

They have four suppliers, covering these areas:

Absolute Systems have provided most of the EPOS Systems equipment that are re-sold, and have a large and profitable traditional maintenance contract in place as well as gaining a lot of good business through add-ons and upgrades.

They also have good capability in supplying IT infrastructure and could respond to a request to supply voice infrastructure although technically they are not strong in this area. Their Contact Centre experience is minimal.

Absolute have extremely good relationships with the CEO, CFO and CTO as well as technical engineers.

BetaComp are very strong in IT and traditional voice infrastructure and currently maintain the majority of the in-house estate, as well as getting about three quarters of the add-ons and upgrades that become available.

They have strong relationships with the CIO, IT staff in general and senior managers in procurement.

They have a good but quite technically different Contact Centre solution that would give ShopSys some advantages, but would mean a lot of operational upheaval.

ContactaCorp are a specialist Contact Centre supplier and incumbent in ShopSys, supplying and maintaining the majority of the Contact Centre system and applications.

They have excellent relationships with Sales and Marketing management and good relationships with the Contact Centre management team and with the CFO.

They have no capability outside of Contact Centre.

Deltamann are a young but fast growing 'Communications Integrator' who claim to provide 'total solutions' in the IT and voice markets, as well as having some expertise in specialist areas including EPOS hardware.

They have a small number of in-depth relationships with the CIO and CTO and are currently engaged to write the Business Case for a massive upgrade of the Contact Centre; as part of this they are openly able to bid for the eventual project, and will be very well placed to win that business because of their relationships with the IT team, and deep knowledge of the requirements.

Deltamann are also currently bidding to do a large consulting project with the EPOS Design & Development Team, developing the cloud based proposition and are developing good relationships with senior technical management.

In addition they have also just acquired a medium sized IT infrastructure reseller, and are keen to look for opportunities within ShopSys.

Imagining that the above is common knowledge to all of the companies involved, what would be your overall sales strategy if you were the Account Manager in each of these cases?

There are no 'right' or 'wrong' answers to Case Examples such as this, which are designed to help in thinking through classic situations, which sometimes get clouded when you have the myriad amounts of data in a real life account. You can go to www.realaccountplanning.com/Cases to read a selection of model responses and also to make your own comments.

Reviewing Account Plans

Reviewing of Account Plans is a critical aspect in ensuring maximum benefit is gained from the whole exercise, and while reviewing the plan yourself is good (using the 'challenges' previously described) more can be achieved by having other people involved.

Plans are reviewed all the time in many organisations, and while some are very effective, a good many are either a complete waste of time and in some cases actually counter productive. They can make irrelevant or ill considered comments, insist upon changes that are not in the best interests of the team (or indeed the company) and can be demoralising if not handled well.

The most common mistake that people make is in not having clarity about the aims of the Account Plan Review. Many outcomes are possible and valid; for example in the case of the Sales Manager of the real Account Manager these might be:

- *Education*: for their own general education on the account situation and plan

- *Control*: in order to check out progress towards goals and objectives as part of Performance Management

- *Decisions:* understanding resource requests, so that decisions can be made for example the use of pre-sales technical resources

- *Direct improvement*: to give direct instructions as to how the account should be handled, especially in the case of junior Account Managers (as perceived by Reviewer)

- *Coaching:* to give constructive feedback that will help the Account Team to improve the plan; perhaps to act as a sounding board for some alternate approaches

Whatever their objectives, any reviewer should be clear in their own mind what it is that they are trying to achieve, and this should be communicated to the Account Manager. For their part a real Account Manager will insist on understanding what each reviewer is trying to achieve (often forcing the reviewer to think it through), and will also be clear what he or she and the rest of the Account Team want to achieve. In this case the objectives of the real Account Manager may include:

- *Approval:* ensuring that key stakeholders, including senior management are comfortable with the Plan

- *Resource allocation:* getting particular people, budgets or other precious resources assigned to the Account Team

- *Setting expectations:* so that management and others know what is likely to be achieved in the account over what timescales; in practice you have to be very careful with this as the session can turn into a negotiation over targets and forecast (see later section for a specific discussion about Account Plan Objectives and Target Setting)

- *Coaching:* to get feedback on the plan which will help to refine and improve it; to gain different perspectives, uncovering any blind spots or other areas of opportunity

Whatever their objectives, the real Account Manager will state them clearly to the Reviewing Team and gain agreement that they are fair and valid, fitting in with the Reviewer's own aims.

As stated, many Account Plan Review sessions are a waste of time, and the primary reason being that the attendees were not clear on what they were trying to achieve, and so it simply becomes a 'talking shop'.

Questions to ask during Account Reviews

An Account Review session by its nature should be a fluid and dynamic experience, however being prepared with good questions in advance can go a long way to helping it to achieve outcomes. Some questions that you might want to ask during a review session include:

During initial preliminaries

- Who else has been involved in developing this Plan?

- Have you involved anyone from the customer in this exercise?

- Have you involved anyone from any other interested third party / partner (channel Business Partner, consultant, vendor etc.)?

During Situation Analysis regarding the client business

- What keeps the CEO awake at night?

- What are the key Business Change Imperatives (Critical Success Factors) for this business?

- What are the main Operational Factors (Accelerators / Inhibitors), impacting the BCI's?

- How would their key competitors / benchmark organisations describe them?

During Situation Analysis regarding the Playing Field

- Where are our Single Points of contact and vulnerability?

- Who do we not know about <a particular person>?

- How can we be sure about the mapping?

- Do we know where our competitors are aligned?

- What evidence do we have that <person> is telling the truth?

- What are the personal agendas of the Key Players?

- Do we have at least one strong Supporter in the core Decision Making Unit?

- Do we have an appropriate plan for Management/Executive engagement?

- Do we have an appropriate plan for 'High and Wide' engagement?

Real Account Planning

- Who in the Playing Field has been promoted in the last twelve months?

- Are there any external consultants involved in the Playing Field; how are they aligned; what is their agenda?

During Situation Analysis regarding Our Competitors

- Are we focusing on the correct strategic competitors?

- Do we really understand their political alignment and their Strategies?

- Are we being overly pessimistic / optimistic?

- Where do you think new competitors will emerge from in this account?

- What other Business Partners / channel / routes to market do they use for similar products and services to ours?

- Have you taken into account the long period of relationship building that they have engaged in – what does this buy them?

During discussion on the Goal Statement

- What alternatives did you consider?

- What were your reasons for choosing this particular Goal statement?

- How does this reflect the account standing in our segmentation model?

- Is the Goal suitably stretching and over an appropriate timescale?

During discussion of Objectives

- Are these SMART? (Specific, Measurable, Achievable, Relevant, Timed)

- Why have you not stretched yourself more / less?

- Will achieving these Objectives lead to our Goal?

- How are these integrated with your Strategies?

During discussion of Strategies

- What other Strategies did you consider and decide not to adopt?
- Have you covered all of the PROFT (Positioning, Relationships, Operational, Financial, Technology) elements?
- Where are our strategies strong?
- Where do our strategies contain exposures?

During discussion of Tactics

- How do these Tactics integrate as part of your Strategies?
- Is everyone firmly committed to carrying out these actions?
- Do you have resources / bandwidth to realistically complete the Tactics?
- Have we identified 'Ultra High Leverage' Tactics i.e. easy / low cost to implement but high impact on the customer?

During discussion on the Conclusions

- Have all the assumptions been identified?
- What other major risks are foreseen?
- How does the risk / reward for this account compare with others?
- What are the Critical Success Factors for us in this account?
- What would our key competitor do if they knew the detail of our plan?
- How would we respond?

In Appendix 4 the ProAct Business Development recommended review process is reproduced, showing that to be successful the session needs a little more organising than a simple meeting. The key points to bear in mind are:

- Get the right people to attend

- Make sure that everyone is well prepared beforehand

- Be clear on the aims and expected outcomes of the session

- Have a process and stick to it (consider having an external Facilitator to manage the process and ensure relevant contributions from all attendees)

- Get the Account Manager and Account Team to present their plan with 'questions of clarification only' during an early part of the review process

- Ensure that you get both positive and constructively negative comments; the Support and Challenge approach works well (I would like to Support you on… and would Challenge you on..)

- If possible get concrete suggestions for improvement during the session

- Document the outcome

- Make sure that the whole process is supportive of the Account Manager and the Account Team who must get real value from it; otherwise there will be a real struggle to repeat the process

- Schedule follow-up sessions in a reasonable time period so that it becomes an on-going process

Communicating the Plan

For many real Account Managers, one of the primary aims of having a well thought through, succinct and documented plan is so that they can communicate the relevant parts of what may have been in their head, to everyone who is involved in the account.

Security of Information

In all aspects of communicating the plan, please bear in mind that not only is there much confidential information contained in the plan, there are also details of your proposed actions. All this information would be valuable to not just direct competitors, but also some Business Partners, suppliers of complementary products (external and perhaps internal) and others.

Your company wide processes and systems should address issues of information security, but Account Managers and others in the core Account Team also need to be very aware of the factors involved.

Notwithstanding the security issues, there may be a large number of people that should get some form of communication:

The Core Account Team

As has been discussed, best practice is for the core Account Team to be intimately involved in crafting the plan, and for them the final written version is just a record of what they have agreed. There should be little need for a formal communication of the plan to this core team of a handful of people, yet it is probably a good idea to make sure that they have read and agree with the very final version of the plan. It is amazingly easy for a small group of tightly knit individuals to go through a rigorous process, and yet still at the end when presented with the documented plan to pick up areas where they don't agree that what is written down fairly represents what they thought had been agreed.

In practice it is always useful to force the core Account Team to re-read the final version and while they may not have to 'sign in blood' you will want some formal agreement, so as to avoid the "that's not what we meant by..." or "I only said we would try to do it by that date .. I didn't give a commitment".

Immediate Management

Immediate Management obviously means the Sales Manager that the Account Manager reports to, but may also include local Pre-Sales Management, Delivery Management and others.

These people may well be familiar with the account, and it is often the case that you will have involved them in some part of the planning process.

They are going to be interested in the Account Plans for a number of reasons, including:

- As a vehicle for coaching the Account Manager and others

- To enable them to allocate and control resources more effectively

- As part of their background development of knowledge about their business

There is another reason that some Managers are interested in Account Plans and that is to help them with allocating sales targets. This is dealt with specifically in the next section, but the bottom line is: *Don't confuse Account Planning and Target Setting*; they are two separate exercises for totally separate reasons.

While good Account Planning can inform effective Target Setting (and vice versa) the risk of contamination is so high that you should totally divorce these two activities as far as possible.

If your immediate management are not able to separate out Account Planning and Target Setting, then in practice a real Account Manager will have to be very careful in communicating the plan and especially the numbers; whenever this happens it is a huge shame for which the Sales Manager should take responsibility.

In the majority of healthy environments immediate management will take a responsible and mature attitude towards the plan. They will be extremely interested in their top accounts and will have been involved throughout. In communicating the plan good real Account Managers will seek help, support and challenges to help them improve overall.

The Wider Account Team

Outside the handful of individuals in the Core Account Team there will probably be many more who touch the customer in some way, including other pre-sales specialists, consultants, installation and service people, credit controllers, customer training specialists and many others.

It will have been impractical to have included them in the actual Account Planning sessions, but they need to understand the plan, and hopefully buy into it.

A good real Account Manager will have involved this group to a certain extent already, either directly by going to them for input and advice, or indirectly for example by a lead pre-sales technical consultant polling the views of others in the technical community.

When presenting the plan to this group the real Account Team has to strike a careful balance between on the one hand communicating a definite, committed plan and on the other hand not appearing to be dictatorial and out of touch. Where time permits you have probably already shared drafts of the plan, or drafts of particular sections of the plan with the wider team, particularly the 'opinion formers' within the various sub-groups.

Striking an appropriate tone appears to be important, for example opening the presentation of the Account Plan and stressing

- You have taken a wide range of views into account

- Sometimes differing views had to be resolved

- You and the core Account Team have thought long and hard about the Goals, Objectives, Strategies and Tactics and come up with what you genuinely believe to be the optimal plan for the organisation

- No plan is ever complete and perfect, and you will keep refining it in light of experience and inputs from everyone involved

- Your objective in communicating the plan is for everyone to understand the context in which they are operating in this account, and for them to be able to play their part as an important part of a wider team

Clearly you will want to communicate the plan succinctly but in an appropriate level of detail, and many real Account Managers will ask for questions and comments, and then gain commitment from the wider team by asking them explicitly to follow the Plan in all of their dealings with this particular customer.

Senior Management

The reason for senior executives reviewing an Account Plan is often different from that of the immediate manager. They are generally not primarily concerned with coaching the team or making resource decisions, more often they want to:

- Have a sense check; are we managing the account effectively

- Getting to understand what is happening at ground level and in the real world

- Briefing themselves so that they can add value in any executive engagement

We know that senior managers, just like everyone else, come in all different types with many different attitudes and approaches, but as a real Account Manager it is maybe worth reflecting on the more common traits of senior executives:

- More externally focused than mid level operational management (what is happening in the market, with competitors, with Business Partners)

- Will look out and plan over longer timescales

- Understand and are used to managing in ambiguity

- More focused on bottom line outcomes and what it means for the business

- Understanding that it is normally much more effective to take colleagues with them; they want to know that 'my people are comfortable with this'

- Have shorter attention spans

- Regard a good meeting as one where there are firm action outcomes

Bearing the above in mind, when communicating with senior management, as with all communications you will firstly understand what their aim is for the session, what they want to get out of it, and what style they will appreciate.

In general, when communicating the Account Plan to senior management real Account Managers will:

- Keep the formal presentation short and succinct

- Do their homework and have plenty of back up data in case there is a deep dive into a particular aspect

- Allow plenty of time for discussion, keeping it interactive and conversational

- Have clear outcomes that they want to achieve; and will gain agreement on these outcomes (for example agreement to actions, funding, access to others)

Business Partners and other third parties

Later in this book there are sections dealing with Joint Planning with Business Partners and others involved in the account, which is a great activity to get engaged in, but which requires excellent relationships and trust.

There will be many situations where developing the plan with a Business Partner may not be feasible, desired or physically possible. In these cases some form of communication of the plan will often be appropriate, however the real Account Manager has to balance two factors that are often conflicting:

- The desire to be open, honest and trustworthy with the Business Partner, and to give them enough information to have a good context within which they can operate effectively with your Account Team

- The need to protect yourself, including restricting the information given to the Business Partner, who may often be pursuing slightly different goals than yourself

It is not possible to be prescriptive about communicating with Business Partners and other third parties, however the one finding from observing many excellent real Account Managers is that they give this matter a great deal of thought. They do not automatically assume that they have to share everything with the Business Partner and then get disappointed when the partner acts only in their own best interest, nor do they assume that the Business Partner is not capable of working effectively together and so it is best to keep them totally in the dark.

Experience is a great teacher in this regard, and great real Account Managers ensure that they get good experience directly and through others, for example by talking with any Business Partner Account Manager, discussing with colleagues who have worked with the particular Business Partner recently, and being prepared to develop relationships over time, steadily trying to move closer together where it is possible and makes sense.

With the Customer

As with Business Partners, the issue of Joint Planning with customers is covered in the next section. If you are not in a position to do joint planning, there may be merit in sharing the plan or at least parts of the plan, with your customer.

Experienced real Account Managers have recounted that when doing this it is best to:

- Choose the individuals carefully; in general they would be true Supporters that you know you can trust

- Do not give them the whole plan, but only sections of it; potentially slightly altered to suit the situation

- Asking customers to help develop or verify the Situation Analysis can be especially useful

- The Business Characteristics part of a real Account Plan can be a really good tool to help gain access to or nurture relationships with senior executives; in which case you might actually expand this section of the plan (at least for that conversation, even if you then summarise it for your internal plan)

- Where possible do not rely on one individual for information

- In general it is best not to give copies of internal and especially work-in-progress documents to customers, as however well meaning they can subsequently get mis-used

Although careful thought is again required before communicating the real Account Plan with customers, it can be tremendously powerful, allowing you not only to get valuable inside information, but also in itself generating and nurturing relationships which can help enormously in developing business for mutual benefit.

Account Planning and Target Setting

Some Sales Managers and some Account Managers confuse Account Planning and Target Setting. They are two very different exercises and are best kept very separate. There are some linkages, which get discussed at the end of this section, but these are really a by-product of the two processes.

Real Account Planning is about the Account Team analysing the current situation, deciding where they want to take the relationship and then creatively coming up with approaches and actions that will get them there. To be a great real Account Manager requires the ability to be proactive and as in Star Trek to boldly go where no one has gone before.

Target Setting is in itself a confused practice. Great sales organisations realise that the only reason that you set targets for sales people and Account Managers is to motivate behaviours and being clear on expectations.

Target setting for Account Managers should not simply be an exercise in making numbers add up to meet some business objective. Clearly there is some relationship between the achievements that are reasonably expected from an Account Manager and the company business plan, but to simply make them add up to the same number is simply either being lazy or not understanding what sales management is all about.

It is critical to the success of any Account Planning programme that Sales Managers at all levels separate out the development and refinement of great Plans from target setting, otherwise both processes will get severely polluted, often to the point where they become irrelevant as the protagonists simply involve themselves in game playing.

Summary

- *The planning process is often as important as the actual physical plan*

- *Segmentation of accounts based on current performance and future potential*

- *You need to make it your own*

- *Challenge your Account Plans*

- *Use the Ten Tests*

- *Set up and use intelligent Account Reviews*

- *Use the Plan as a communication and co-ordination tool*

- *Don't confuse Account Planning and Target Setting*

PART 5: BUSINESS PARTNER PLANNING & JOINT PLANNING

"Any intelligent fool can make things bigger and more complex... It takes a touch of genius - and a lot of courage to move in the opposite direction."

Albert Einstein

"Keep your friends close, and your enemies closer still"

Niccolò Machiavelli in The Prince

Planning for Business Partners

By Business Partner we refer to resellers, integrators, dealers or other organisations who sell to end users on your behalf or alongside you to offer a total solution. They are not interested in your product or service in itself, but as a means of them making money either directly by selling your offering, or indirectly by selling complementary products or services to deliver a total solution to their customer.

Generally the actual delivered solution will flow through them, although increasingly they may earn a 'margin' through a commission or other device.

Just as in selling to end users where there are Account Managers who are not really managing their accounts in Business Partner or Channel Sales there is a similar difference between individuals who simply facilitate, maintain and service a relationship (we could hardly call them sales people) and real Business Partner Account Managers who proactively develop the relationship, including developing new business streams.

The need for real Account Planning is arguably stronger in Business Partner relationships as you will normally have less accounts and generally they leverage your business more. In many cases the loss of an end-user account would be bad but they can be replaced, whereas it may be more difficult and in some geographies or verticals impossible to replace a Business Partner.

Real Account Planning is a similar process for Business Partner selling, and will follow the Where-are-we-now, Where-do-we-want-to-be-in-the-future, and How-will-we-get-there approach of direct end-user real Account Management, embodied in the SA-GOST process and tools.

There are however some slight differences in all elements:

Situation Analysis with Business Partners:

Good practice will still be to look at the Business Partner as a business, our competition and the Playing Field (organisation chart plus), however in addition real Business Partner Account Managers will also consider:

- The Business Partner's own Business Plan
- Especially how they segment their market
- Their target and growth areas
- Market propositions
- How they differentiate themselves

In the Situation Analysis and especially the Playing Field it is normally useful to consider the three separate decisions that the Business Partner real Account Manager is trying to get in his or her favour:

Partner Entry Level Decisions

This is the initial decision by the Business Partner to engage with a particular vendor. It is often a strategic decision based on an investment being made by the Business Partner in training, marketing, service and support capability; it can sometimes also be a tactical decision if there is little particular investment required, and if there is a large opportunity available.

Entry Level Decisions are typically made at higher levels in the company, with a champion driving through the process (alternatively it could be sales led for a tactical opportunity based entry).

The output of the Entry Level Decision is that you are able to start developing pro-active business with this Business Partner.

It is essential to every selling organisation that you have a well thought through process for selecting new Business Partners in a geography, vertical or solution area. The process of gaining entry into a new Business Partner will normally be a two-way one with both parties agreeing a business proposition.

Partner Promotion Level Decisions

Having taken the decision to work with a particular vendor, Business Partners will then decide which particular ones they will promote within their organisation and to their customers. Many Business Partners will have a formal or informal tiering of preferred and secondary vendors.

These decisions are typically made in the Marketing organisation (Product Marketing or Propositions Management), and would involve further commitment of resources to building business with a vendor through joint activities, co-marketing, demonstration / Proof of Concept (POC) facilities etc.

The outcome of Promotion Level Decisions are that your products and services are much more likely to be considered seriously by the customer facing teams.

Partner Bid Level Decisions

These are decisions made by customer facing teams (sales and pre-sales) often in conjunction with product marketing, to propose a particular vendor into a particular opportunity, and will result in your products and services being bid.

Goals & Objectives with Business Partners

Goals and Objectives with Business Partners will obviously include revenues, but perhaps also items such as:

- Particular product mix
- Design-Wins / Bake-ins
- Wallet share
- Competitive displacement
- Specific market / vertical penetration

- Accreditation levels

- Competency levels of sales people (skills and knowledge)

- Bid rate (how often they bid your offerings against competitors)

And you may also wish to include longer term measures such as

- Partner Gross Margin

- Partner total revenue / EBITDA / net profit

- Attach rate for Partner services / other high-margin offers

- Partner Stickiness, for example by providing a managed service wrap to solutions, or supplying projects on an 'as a service' basis

Strategy with Business Partners

As with direct end user real Account Plans, our strategy statements in a real Business Partner Account Plan will define our overall approach to achieving Goals and Objectives. Again, we deal in strategies because we can choose between alternate ones, which is difficult to do if we go straight to actions.

PROFT (Positioning, Relationships, Operational, Financial and Technology) is still a good checklist to remind us of some key aspects to consider, however with Business Partners we normally consider some other factors and determine appropriate strategies.

Within any Business Partner, there are generally only two high level approaches that you could adopt to increasing revenues:

Competitive Knockout

Where the Business Partner has an existing and projected revenue spend on a certain class of product or service, which currently they satisfy with a competitive vendor.

With Competitive Knockout you will generally be looking to demonstrate a superior proposition to the Business Partner than that offered by your competitors. For example this could be:

- Increased retained margins
- Greater differentiation
- Easier (less costly) selling
- More opportunity to sell other value-add and profitable products or services
- Better account control

Incremental opportunity

Incremental opportunity assumes that there are possibilities to develop new profitable revenue potential within the Business Partner, typically by helping them to develop new markets and revenue / margin streams. Your approach here will be to work with the Business Partner to identify and build new propositions backed up by internal business plans which open up increased revenue, margin and profit potential to the Business Partner at an acceptable level of risk.

While the actual strategies for achieving your Goals and Objectives will be unique to every Business Partner, there are a number of common strategies that may provide 'food for thought' in helping to craft your own approach.

Dominance Strategy: this is an all out approach to gaining total control of the Business Partner. It will always include an element of Relationship based strategy. This strategy is resource intensive to implement but can result in high levels of predictable business. This strategy will require great levels of adaptability in tactics, as it means that you will respond to each and every change in the Business Partner situation and competitive activity. A Dominance Strategy will at some point become very transparent to the Business Partner, who will have to make a strategic decision themselves as to whether or not their business is best served by this type of approach. Will they be prepared to 'put all their eggs in one basket' in return for greater levels of co-operation, trust, marketing funds or potential margin?

Segmentation Strategy: this strategy is to secure broad areas of the Business Partner activity, which can then be defended. The areas that you will want to capture will often be organisational (e.g. a particular division), geographic (e.g. Western business), or application oriented (e.g. all in-store business).

Guerrilla Strategy: this strategy is very opportunistic and is characterised by liberal canvassing across the entire Business Partner for available opportunities and then tactically responding to them as they occur. A Guerrilla strategy can work well in a new Business Partner, particularly where there is a strong incumbent supplier.

Typically a Guerrilla strategy will depend on strong relationships at the sales level (Bid Decisions). These could be built on specific opportunities working with sales people, or often by finding technical pre-sales specialists who will champion your technology. The continuing success of a Guerrilla strategy will normally drive the central areas to build a more stable and deeper relationship with you.

In the majority of cases a Guerrilla strategy will evolve into some other approach over time, once sufficient footholds have been established and understanding of the Business Partner improved.

Withdrawal: Often overlooked by sales people, in many cases the optimal strategy is Withdrawal, either from a particular opportunity or position, or ultimately from the Business Partner itself. Withdrawal will obviously require careful qualification, however should never be overlooked as an option - remember we want to win the war and win the peace, this does not necessarily mean winning every battle; great real Account Planning is about giving yourself choice.

In addition to your overall strategy with a Business Partner, in the majority of cases your strategy statements will include:

Propositions Plan: in many cases the propositions that a particular Business Partner will supply or re-market are straight forward, however it is often worthwhile examining where the unique capabilities that both organisations possess can be combined into new unique joint solutions or propositions to attack a particular segment of the overall market.

Marketing Plan: how your marketing efforts will be synergistic; how the Business Partner can take advantage of particular campaigns and events that you have planned and vice versa.

Provision of Proof Plan: the Provision of Proof will enable the Business Partner to effectively convince their customers of the validity of solutions that include your offerings. This will traditionally include demonstration equipment, and now includes reference case studies, access to proof of concept facilities, access to remote demonstration capability etc.

Sales Enablement Plan: how you will ensure that all of the relevant individuals in the Business Partner are trained and motivated to sell and support your propositions, above other competitors. As well as formal training you will often include informal coaching, other development activities and motivation such as rewards and recognition of individuals, teams and the whole company.

Technical Support Plan: to ensure technical excellence and how the Business Partner can interface effectively with your technical departments, both pre and post sales.

Buying Service Plan: the 'buying service' is the term used by some vendors to describe how they will make the whole process of the transaction as smooth, quick, accurate and efficient as possible. In many cases Business Partners know exactly what they want to procure and no selling is involved; so how can you orchestrate the situation and your own organisation to make sure that this happens effectively?

Channel Plan: in many cases it will be possible for the Business Partner direct relationship to be through one or a number of other channels. Typically this would be some form of distributor, but could involve other resellers or agents. Real Account Managers will carefully choose the optimal channel route for each Business Partner, taking into account issues such as support requirements, margin allocation, financial risk (credit), the potential for non-authorised channels to become involved, physical delivery requirements, joint business development activities and overall levels of trust.

Common Mistakes

Practically all vendors who work through 'channels' have some form of 'Joint Account Plan' in place, yet many of them are not really 'plans' and certainly not real Business Partnership Development Plans. An analysis of a number of 'Joint Plans' by vendors in the IT, Software and Telecoms sectors, revealed a number of common mistakes:

- Only numbers driven (the numbers are important but they are the Objectives of the real Plan)

- Tactical by nature; often a series of short term 'initiatives' for example specific promotions

- Not looking at where the relationship is headed in the medium term, for example no alignment as to markets to address and winning propositions

- No senior management commitment; plans are often agreed by mid level managers in each party, and then destroyed by some change in strategy at a higher level

- Too narrow a focus; often looking solely at the particular solutions offered by the vendor, without looking at the wider impact on the Business Partner and how they differentiate / position themselves, how they make an overall good blended margin and how they develop their business overall

- Too generic; plans in practice just focus on what we have termed Promotion Decisions which create a good climate for the vendor and Business Partner to do business together, however by themselves do not actually generate business. It is also necessary to impact actual specific Bid Decisions, where the Business Partner is deciding on which vendor to align with in certain customer situations (and when the Vendor is deciding on which Business Partner to align with)

- Too specific; similar to being too short term, many planning sessions focus entirely on driving current identified opportunities (either specific customers or market positions) and do not take attempt to look wider at other possibilities for mutual benefit

- Business veneer only; many of the 'business planning' sessions that have been observed are little more than a short meeting to agree targets and incentives (rebates etc.). There is no attempt to understand longer term context or business challenges, understand and develop relationships between the organisations, discuss mutually beneficial processes or any of the other areas that would normally be covered in a real Account Planning session

Joint Account Planning of End-user Customers with Business Partners

In many instances vendors, integrators, dealers, service partners, consultants and others are working together on the same account. Sometimes the relationships are formal and well understood, sometimes that are less formal, fluid and can be ambiguous.

The majority of this book examines developing your own real Account Plan to proactively develop business within an account. Where you are working closely with other organisations, there is often benefit in doing some form of Joint Planning.

If there is close alignment, for example between a vendor and a Business (Channel) Partner, then the Joint Plan can follow the standard best practice already outlined, in both the process and the end plan format itself.

If the alignment is very loose and not fully understood or committed to by both sides, then there may still be some merit in a form of joint planning, but you will have to be satisfied with only a partial plan, which will not replace your own comprehensive plan.

Case Study: Joint Partner Program

The Joint Partner Programme is run by a major global software company, following a successful series of Account Planning workshops that they had implemented across Europe.

Their issue was that although they had good visibility, control and growth plans for their very major accounts which they account managed directly, in their second tier of accounts, where they had deployed 'High Touch' Account Managers working with a channel of accredited Business Partners, they believed that they were missing opportunities.

Typically in these accounts the solution supplied was a single proposition, and although this vendor had many other propositions that could be offered, there was significantly less success with multiple propositions in the second tier accounts.

It was apparent that their channel Business Partners had variable skill and competency levels in terms of Account Management and Account Planning, ranging from quite naive transaction based sales approaches, to some very sophisticated account management teams.

Initially delivered as a pilot programme in one Western European country, the Joint Partner Programme spread across the whole of the company's EMEA Region, and actually evolved into two different types of programmes, with each implementation being further tailored to the particular needs of the Business Partner and the country market.

In essence the programme centred around a two day workshop attended by Account Managers from one carefully chosen Business Partner as well as the vendor's High Touch Account

Managers together with their Technical Account Managers (pre-sales people). Into the workshop were added a number of high level technical and business consultants from the vendor's central European (and in some cases global) teams.

The workshop focused on building and / or refining a real Account Development Plan for a number of pre-qualified customers, where their was a good suspicion that incremental revenue could be generated either by expanding the existing solution into new areas, or by using existing relationships and goodwill to open up possibilities in new application areas.

The two broad flavours of the workshop catered for some instances where the teams needed to be educated and guided through how to build effective plans, versus other situations where real Account Planning principles were well understood, and we could focus exclusively on refining strategies to develop incremental business.

A major part of the time spent was in looking at value creation within the account; mapping their high-level Business Imperatives and Operational Imperatives against real demonstrable value that could be delivered by the vendor and the Business Partner working together.

The workshop concluded with formal presentations of plans and resource requests to senior management from both the Business Partner and the vendor who were able to make resourcing decisions in the workshop. The real Account Plans were then rigorously followed up with regular update and review calls to track progress, ensuring that actions were carried out as well as allowing for a good formal evaluation of the effectiveness of each programme in generating and then closing incremental business.

The results and findings from this particular programme were in line with similar programmes:

- Results can be quite outstanding with very significant incremental possibilities unearthed

- This type of activity only works when there is a reasonable relationship between the two parties, with some level of trust already built up; if this is not the case then neither party is inclined to examine it's own top accounts, and there is a reluctance to be totally open in driving for a common goal

- These kind of initiatives can work well at the Account Manager level, but results are easier to obtain and generally more far-reaching if senior management from both sides are totally committed to the concept

- Having an independent facilitator always helps enormously and is absolutely necessary if there are any issues at all with the general relationship (but your author is biased in this respect)

- A common side benefit is increased efficiency in the account. Whereas previously both the vendor and Business Partner were tending to call on the same group of individuals, with a plan in place they could spread themselves a lot further and avoid overlap in relationships

- Another side benefit is the improved overall inter-personal relationships as well as the knowledge transfer and skills development that goes on with a workshop such as this

- A particular key is in the choice of accounts to put into the programme, with some time spent up front proving to be an invaluable investment

- The final key is to have a rigorous follow-up process, with one reasonably senior individual responsible for ensuring that commitments actually happen

Joint Account Planning with End User Accounts

We have looked at how to create and craft a real Account Plan which drives the business forward to meet the Goals and Objectives that you decide for the account.

In some cases you may want to develop this further with a Joint Plan agreed with the customer.

A word of warning in that it is extremely unusual to have a situation where you can arrive at an all encompassing Joint Plan which covers all aspects of the relationship, and where you would not want to have at least a partial Plan of your own. There are several reasons for this including:

- Most sizeable accounts cannot be regarded as one entity; for example in the IT world it is common to have different relationships with the central IT Group, with business units, with the procurement function and perhaps with decentralised IT groups. It may be possible to develop a Joint Plan with one of these groups, perhaps with two groups, but rarely with all the various constituent parts

- However good the relationship, there is always some divergence of goals; again it may be possible and desirable to build a Plan to cover the areas of common goals, but there will then need to be separate plans for other areas

- Even with a fantastic relationship, a perfect symmetry of Goals, and a Plan that is totally committed to by both parties, a real Account Manager will still wish to separately consider contingency plans in the event that key individuals were to move on from their current positions, or the organisation was suddenly to face either new unforeseen challenges (or opportunities) brought about by for example changes in their markets or through mergers and acquisitions

So while a true all encompassing Joint Account Plan may be very difficult and often impossible to achieve, there are other options that can also give tremendous benefits, and which the real Account Manager will consider:

- Asking key individuals to help with preparation of the Plan, in particular the Situation Analysis and company background

- Sharing key parts of the plan with certain individuals, particularly Supporters or Agents

- Asking Supporters or Agents to discuss with the Account Manager any critical aspects of the Plan, especially how others would respond

- Carving out particular aspects of the Plan and creating separate Joint Plans. For example you may be somewhat ambivalent with regard to the Technology strategy, but parts of the customer may care passionately about this; a natural approach would be to set up a workshop to develop a Joint Plan for this element only

Facilitating the Joint Planning session

If you have decided to develop either a full or partial real Account Plan with your customer or channel Business Partner, there are a number of points that have been found to be critical for success:

- Make sure that you have all interpersonal relationships in good shape before the start of the exercise

- Don't have Enemies (someone else's Agent or strong Supporter) attend, as they will sabotage the process either during the event or subsequently

- Be clear at the start on what you are trying to achieve:

  - What are the boundaries of the Plan?

  - How the output of the session will be regarded; for example will it be binding on both parties, will it be seen as recommendations only?

  - How you will measure the quality and success of the eventual outcome?

- Keep the number of people involved low and to the Core Teams only; you can communicate or involve others later; four to six people in total is an optimal number with normally a maximum of eight participants

- Wherever possible have an independent person facilitate the process; ideally this would be an external consultant who understands the environment of the vendor and customer and whose fees would be paid jointly by the two parties

Summary

- *Creating a real Account Plan for a Business Partner can follow a very similar process to planning for end-user customers*

- *With Business Partners we normally consider:*
    - *Entry Level Decisions*
    - *Promotion Level Decisions*
    - *Bid Level Decisions*

- *Business Partners represent ideal opportunities to do Joint Planning*

- *This can extend to joint planning of end user opportunities and accounts*

- *Joint planning with end-user accounts is also possible, but the scope and reality of the plan needs to be considered*

- *Give careful consideration to the process of running any joint planning session*

APPENDICES

The following contains some resources, which are offered as examples for you to start experimenting with crafting excellent real Account Plans.

Unless otherwise noted tools presented are all copyright © ProAct Business Development LLC or in some cases © Links Development.

ProAct and Links Development licences all readers to use these tools for their own evaluation purposes only. Please contact ProAct or Links Development for further information about how to licence the tools for widespread use.

No warranty is given or liability accepted for use of these tools.

Electronic copies of these tools are available from www.realaccountplanning.com

Appendix 1: MAP3

An example template for a standard Account Plan

The MAP3 (Managing Accounts Proactively) Account Development Plan template from ProAct Business Development is an example of a GOST based plan, suitable for a mid level account.

ProAct has given permission for readers to use these tools for their own personal use, but not to distribute these materials in any way, and not for widespread, systematic usage. ProAct will be pleased to discuss with you commercial licensing of their suite of Account Planning tools. Contact info@proactbd.org

MAP3 Account Development Plan *for:*

Prepared by	
With	
Executive Sponsor	
Reviewed by	
On	
Next review due	

MAP3 Account Development Plan

ProAct
Business Development

Topics

Introduction

Where we are now
- **Situation Analysis**
  - **Account Characteristics**
  - **Playing Field**
  - **Competition**
- **Overall Relationship**
- **SWOT & SWOT Plus**

Where we want to get to
- **Goal and Business Objectives**

How we will get there
- **Strategies**
- **Milestones**
- **Tactics**
- **Key Player Mapping**

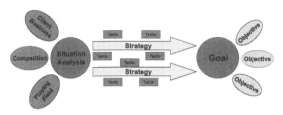

Plan overview
- **Our Proposition**
- **Assumptions & Risks**
- **CSF's**
- **Actions required**
- **Q & A; Discussion**
- **Summary**

MAP3 Account Development Plan

Part 1

Where We Are Now

The Situation Analysis

Client Business, Our Competition, The Playing Field, SWOT & SWOT Plus, Overall Relationship

MAP3 Account Development Plan

Basic Account Information

Account name

Parent

Affiliates

FY starts

Description of their business

MAP3 Account Development Plan

ProAct
Business Development

Basic Account Information

	Revenue	Profit (NEAT)	Assets	Employees
Last FY				
Previous FY				
Change				

Profit / Revenue	Profit / Assets (ROA)	Profit / Employee
Change in last year	Change in last year	Change in last year
%	%	
Industry average	Industry average	Industry average

General description of the account and our relationship

MAP3 Account Development Plan

ProAct
Business Development

Business Characteristics

Their mission / charter

They measure success by

Their Key Drivers are

Their customer proposition is

Their competitive position is described as

MAP3 Account Development Plan

ProAct
Business Development

The organisation in its market

Strengths	Weaknesses
Opportunities	Threats

MAP3 Account Development Plan

ProAct
Business Development

Our competitive positioning

Our top competitor is	*Our second competitor is*
Their past relationship	*Their past relationship*
Their Supporters are	*Their Supporters are*
Their likely Goal and Objectives are	*Their likely Goal and Objectives are*
Their likely Strategies are	*Their likely Strategies are*
Their Strengths are	*Their Strengths are*
Their Exposures are	*Their Exposures are*

MAP3 Account Development Plan

ProAct
Business Development

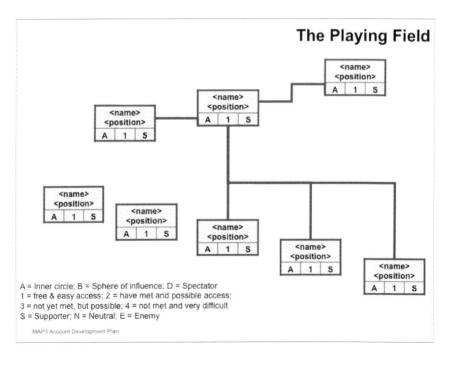

The Playing Field

A = Inner circle; B = Sphere of influence; D = Spectator
1 = free & easy access; 2 = have met and possible access;
3 = not yet met, but possible; 4 = not met and very difficult
S = Supporter; N = Neutral; E = Enemy

MAP3 Account Development Plan

Buying Patterns

	P-8	P-7	P-6	P-5	P-4	P-3	P-2	P-1	This
Total ICT spend									
Our total addressable spend									
Our revenues									
Our rev. / total spend	#DIV/0!	#DIV/0!	#DIV/0!	#DIV/0!	#DIV/0!	#DIV/0!	#DIV/0!	#DIV/0!	#DIV/0!
Our rev. / addressable spend	#DIV/0!	#DIV/0!	#DIV/0!	#DIV/0!	#DIV/0!	#DIV/0!	#DIV/0!	#DIV/0!	#DIV/0!
<competitor 1> revenues									
Rev. / addressable spend	#DIV/0!	#DIV/0!	#DIV/0!	#DIV/0!	#DIV/0!	#DIV/0!	#DIV/0!	#DIV/0!	#DIV/0!
<competitor 2> revenues									
Rev. / addressable spend	#DIV/0!	#DIV/0!	#DIV/0!	#DIV/0!	#DIV/0!	#DIV/0!	#DIV/0!	#DIV/0!	#DIV/0!

MAP3 Account Development Plan

ProAct
Business Development

SWOT: Our relationship

Strengths	Weaknesses
Opportunities	**Threats**

MAP3 Account Development Plan

ProAct
Business Development

Part 2

Where We Want to Get To

Goal & Objectives

The Goal Statement & SMART end Business Objectives

MAP3 Account Development Plan

Goal & Business Objectives

> ### *<Goal Statement>*

SMART end Business Objectives
- **x**

MAP3 Account Development Plan

Part 3

How We Will Get There

Strategy & Tactics

Strategies, Tactics, Milestones, Key Player Mapper, Opportunity Outlook

MAP3 Account Development Plan

Strategy Statements

Overall
Positioning
Relationships
Operational
Financial
Technology
<Other>

MAP3 Account Development Plan

Strategy Strengths & Exposures

Strategy Strengths ✔

Strategy Exposures ✖

MAP3 Account Development Plan

ProAct
Business Development

Milestones

Our SMART Milestone Objectives

MAP3 Account Development Plan

ProAct
Business Development

Tactical Action Plan

Description	Who	When	Comments/Outcome

MAP3 Account Development Plan

ProAct
Business Development

Key Player Mapper

Name	Position	I	A	O	Our contact

I : Influence : A = Inner circle; B = Sphere of influence; D = Spectator
A : Access : 1 = free & easy access; 2 = have met and possible access;
3 = not yet met, but possible; 4 = not met and very difficult access
O : Orientation : S = Supporter; N = Neutral; E = Enemy

MAP3 Account Development Plan

ProAct
Business Development

Opportunity Outlook

Description	Value	When	Buy Cycle	Comments

ProAct
Business Development

MAP3 Account Development Plan

Part 4

Plan Overview

Conclusions, Questions & Summary

CSF's, Assumptions, Risks

MAP3 Account Development Plan

Real Account Planning

Critical Success Factors & Asks

Critical Success Factors

Key Asks

MAP3 Account Development Plan

ProAct
Business Development

Plan Conclusions

Assumptions

Risks & Contingencies

Risk	Contingency

MAP3 Account Development Plan

ProAct
Business Development

Real Account Planning

Appendix 2: Business Partner Plan

An example template for a standard Business Partner Account Plan

This example was jointly developed with a global IT hardware and systems vendor, and is tuned to the needs of a channel dealing with medium sized integrators and resellers of their products and services.

Links Development and their particular client have given permission for readers to use these tools for their own personal use, but not to distribute these materials in any way, and not for widespread, systematic usage. Links Development will be pleased to discuss with you commercial usage of this tool or development of templates based on this model. Contact info@linksdev.net

Business Partner
Account Development Plan

<Partner Name>
<date>
<Account Manager>

Business Partner Background

- Business Background
- Capabilities
- Markets
- Finances
- Stakeholder expectations
- Exit Plan (if applicable)
- Growth Plans
- Major Challenges as a business

Our History

- Include revenue and units history over at least last two years
- Include major wins / losses and reference accounts
- Include any major incidents that they would raise
- Include CSAT scores for at least last two years

SWOT on Partner in their Market

Strengths	Weaknesses
Opportunities	Threats

Our Competition

- Other directly competing vendors
  - Strengths & weaknesses
- Other potential competitors
  - Strengths & weaknesses

Wallet Share
(last 4 quarters unless stated otherwise)

Application	Ourselves	Competitor A	Competitor B	Competitor C
App 1				
App 2				
App 3				
Total				

The Playing Field

- Add in all key players
- Colour code BLUE = Entry Decisions
- Green = Promotion Decisions
- RED = Bid Decisions
- Show as Supporter / Neutral / Enemy
- Show importance / influence as
  - A = Inner Circle
  - B = Influencers
  - X = Others

SWOT on Our Relationship

Strengths	Weaknesses
Opportunities	Threats

Goals & Objectives

- How we want to be able to describe the relationship in 12 months

- Specific SMART Objectives

Strategies

-

Tactical Action Plan : Sales

Action	By when	Who	Comments

Tactical Action Plan : Marketing

Action	By when	Who	Comments

Tactical Action Plan : Service Delivery

Action	By when	Who	Comments

Critical Success Factors

• Add in 3 to 5 at most

Appendix 3: The 3+1 Plan

An example of a template for the most succinct plan.

The 3+1 Plan was developed initially for a client who wanted to define the real minimum amount of information that could

be documented and yet still represent a meaningful plan which still encourages the Account Manager to consider the right questions.

The result has proven popular with many Account Managers, particularly where they manage more than a handful of accounts.

The first three slides have proven to be fairly standard for all Account Plans, while the +1 slide is normally modified to reflect the specific metrics / numbers or Key Performance Indicators (KPI's) that are appropriate.

If the 3+1 Plan needs a little more depth, then it can be expanded with +2 or +3 slides or backups covering areas such as:

- Playing Field (organisation chart) and Key Player Analysis
- Expansion of their business characteristics / results
- Competitive commentary (wins, strengths, supporters etc.)
- Identified opportunities (next 12 months)
- Sub plan per major Opportunity
- Player Mapping
- P&L if appropriate
- Major assumptions, risks and contingencies

The example that follows is a completed plan for a sample account.

1   MT plc Account Plan: Situation Analysis

MT plc is the result of a merger some 12 months ago between Myco Plc and Thebig Plc.

Before the merger, Myco were a significant customer of ours. We had built up very strong relationships in both IT and purchasing, and were regarded as the preferred supplier. Thebig was a company on our tier 2 list of suspects, although we have had little success in forming any significant relationships due mainly to the entrenched position of xxxxx.

Key Facts at a glance

Turnover	$840m
Declining	9% p.a.
Profitable	8.1% PBT
Declining	2% p.a.
Employees	11,000

Attached:
Playing Field Analysis

STRENGTHS	WEAKNESSES
• Proven capability for telephony. • Relationships in Home Products. • Account team in place and lots of good contacts. • Good start to a relationship with Jeremy Scott. • Allison James • Our supporters are currently in the ascendancy	• Poor relationship with Group Services & no high level relationship with Group Purchasing. • Rebecca Flood • Whilst we have got good acceptance in HP, they still view us primarily as a base product supplier. • Do not engage with senior management.
OPPORTUNITIES	THREATS
• Potential re-organisation - HP could become an even more Independent Business Unit. • Strong case for consolidation of all Group IT • Veterinary Products?	• Any consolidation of IT / networking would probably introduce new competitors. • Potential re-organisation - leading to greater rationalisation.

© Links Development 2009, 2012

---

2   MT plc Account Plan : Goals, Objectives & Strategies

Goal   **Preferred supplier of communications solutions to the whole group & Trusted Advisor to Home Products Group**

Objectives
- At least $3.2m bookings in next FY
- From start of next calendar year, to secure at least 85% of all voice business
- Minimum one pilot for ABC application.
- All Customer Service Scorecard indicators should be on Green by end of the year

Strategies
- Positioning: Trusted, value for money total communications supplier who can be relied upon to do a good job
- Relationships: Nurturing of at least 2 high level Supporters outside IT. Use the relationships from Remote Access to progress other business. Focus deep relationship building with Home Products IT / Purchasing. Develop relationships throughout the account via mass marketing events (seminars etc).
- Operational: Assign Service Delivery Team with lead Service Delivery Manager. SLA agreed with partner.
- Financial: Compete aggressively in any situation against xxxx, especially in Home Products. Offer per user pricing as soon as possible.
- Technology: Develop a totally compelling value for money and security proposition for all connectivity solutions that we take to senior management within Group. Push to pilot XYZ in one division in next 12 months
- Channel: Agree development plan with current partner or introduce new high end SI

© Links Development 2009, 2012

3   MT plc Account Plan : Tactical Action Plan

Tactical Action Plan   last updated **01-Oct-11**

	Action	Owner	Due date	Status	Notes / Progress
1	Develop draft of internet access proposition	PP	End Oct		Need a team to help draft this
2	Meet with AM & KP to get inputs on draft.	SS	End Oct		
3	Take draft to DC and agree game plan.	SS	End Nov		
4	Initial meet with KM / PS.	SK	End Oct		Objective to gain credibility.
5	Meet JF every month and agree rules of engagement.	SS	On-going		Neutralise
6	Arrange evening senior management roundtable.	SS	End Jan.		Need our top team
7	Formal proposal re internet access to PS.	SK / SS	End Feb		
8	Bi weekly surgeries in Home Products.	NN	On-going		TLC & escalation
9	Six weekly newsletter / mail to all in MT IT & purchasing dept.'s - focus on case studies.	Mkt	On-going		
10	On site seminar on 'Future of communications'.	SS	End Jan		Involve vendors
11	On site seminar on application area.	SS	Feb		Tbd
12	Invite senior managers to corporate hospitality event.	SS	Mar		Tbd - need our top team
13	Sponsor a Xmas shopping trip to Paris for key lower level contacts.	Mkt	Dec.		
14	Set up regular key Executive Sponsorship meetings or calls (see Mapper).	SS	On-going		
15	Weekly internal meet / conference call to pool knowledge.	All	On-going		Thursdays at 8.30
16	6 weekly reviews of the account plan.	SS	On-going		
17					
18					

+1

	FY10	This FY (actual and forecast)					Next FY					FY13	FY14
		Q1	Q2	Q3	Q4	FY11	Q1	Q2	Q3	Q4	FY12		
Revenues							0				0		
Prod1							0				0		
Prod2							0				0		
Prod3							0				0		
Prod4							0				0		
Prod5							0				0		
Prod6							0				0		
Total	0	0	0	0	0	0	0	0	0	0	0	0	0
Resources (days)													
Sales							0				0		
Pre-sales							0				0		
Other							0				0		
Other							0				0		
Spend ($)													
Marketing							0				0		
Other							0				0		
Other							0				0		
Total	0	0	0	0	0	0	0	0	0	0	0	0	0

Other Key Metrics and KPI' s
* xxx

Appendix 4: ProAct's Account Review process

Below is the standard Account Review process developed by ProAct Business Development for their MAP3 (Managing Accounts Proactively) programme. ProAct is happy for you to use this for your own personal use, but not for wider usage; please read the copyright notices at the front of this book.

Account Plan Improvement – the War Room

While every Account Development Plan Improvement session will be unique, and designed to meet the specific business needs of the moment, below is a suggested standard process that can be adapted as appropriate. This is called a 'War Room' and is designed to assist with examining and challenging the current plan together with crafting improvements. If you simply wish to 'review' the plan in terms of management communication and control, then you may prefer to follow the suggested 'Account Plan Review' process outlined on page 121.

Stage 1: Pre-Plan Improvement Session

You should book a good-sized conference room where you will not be interrupted. You will also need other areas or rooms where pairs / trios can work quietly for a few minutes. If possible coffee etc. should be readily available.

The timing of the Plan Improvement is obviously flexible, however most people will find it more productive to schedule Plan Improvements for the start or end of the day. It is suggested that for a 90 minute Plan Improvement, you schedule 2 hours in your diary to allow for over runs, and / or post session discussions.

You should pick the members of the Plan Improvement Team carefully. Obviously you will want the Account Manager and members of the core Account Team to be present. In addition it is useful to have the involvement of any supporting functions (pre sales, service etc.) and perhaps one or two colleagues of the Account Manager, as well as 'management' attendance.

Write to the Account Owner and members of the Improvement Team in advance of the session.

Suggested text to send to Account Owner and Team in advance of the session:

As you know, we have scheduled an Account Development Plan Improvement session (War Room) for <account>, to be held at <time, date, and location>.

The people attending the Plan Improvement session will be <all names>.

The purpose of the session is to allow you to communicate your plan, seek any decisions and support that are appropriate, and most importantly for the plan to be tested through Support and Challenge, so that you are able to keep improving it.

In preparation for the Plan Improvement, can you circulate the current plan to all of the attendees at least < suggest 48 hours > in advance of the session. Can you also prepare a 20-minute overview presentation of your plan, and bring hard copy of any slides that you use, to the session.

If you have any queries or concerns about the Plan Improvement, please do not hesitate to contact me. I am looking forward to this session enormously and hope that we can add real value and help you in this account.

Suggested text to send to Plan Improvement Team in advance of the session:

As you know, we have scheduled an Account Development Plan Improvement session (War Room) for <account>, to be held at <time, date, and location>.

The people attending the Plan Improvement session will be <all names>.

The purpose of the session is to allow the Account Team to communicate their plan, seek any decisions and support that are appropriate, and most importantly for the plan to be tested through Support and Challenge, so that they are able to keep improving it.

You should expect to receive a copy of the plan, at least <days> before the session. During the actual Plan Improvement session, an overview of the plan will be presented, and you will then be asked to prepare Support and Challenge for the plan, and also to come up with suggestions for improvement.

Thank you for your participation in this exercise. If you have any queries or concerns about the Plan Improvement, please do not hesitate to contact me.

Stage 2: The Plan Improvement

A suggested agenda for the Plan Improvement session is described below. This example is for a medium importance account, and assumes that 90 minutes is an appropriate investment of time. Timings can obviously be extended or reduced. It is strongly recommended that you read the Account Development Plan in advance of the session, and make notes of your own observations and suggestions.

Account Development Plan Improvement

Agenda	
0.00	Introduction
	Purpose and agenda (to test and improve the plan)
	Ground Rules (behaviours required including listening, respect, focus on improvement / constructive suggestions and what will drive the business forward, no mobile phones, email or other interruptions)
0.05	Account Development Plan presentation by Account Owner

0.25	Questions of clarification (only)
0.35	The Plan Improvement Team split into pairs / trios and answer the questions:

- What most impresses us about the plan are:

- We would challenge the following aspects :

If there are sufficient people / teams, it is useful to ask different teams to consider the plan from the point of view of the customer / our company / competition / other departments or functions within our company who are significantly impacted (e.g. services function).

The Account Team answer the questions:

- The strongest aspects of our plan are:

- The weakest aspects of our plan are:

To encourage clarity, the teams are required to write bullet points onto flip charts.

0.45	Plenary session where feedback is presented. The Account Team should be first to present, with others presenting only additional items or observations.
1.00	The Plan Improvement Team split into different pairs / trios and answer the questions:

Our Top 3 Suggestions for making the plan even stronger are:...

The Account Team meanwhile considers the feedback that they have been given, and prepares their own suggestions for making the plan stronger.

To encourage clarity, the teams are required to write bullet points onto flip charts.

1.10	Review of suggestions. The Account Team should be first to present, with others presenting only additional suggestions.
	With a small group, the last two steps can be amalgamated into a plenary session, where improvements are brainstormed and evaluated.
1.20	The Account Team summarises what has come out of the session for them.
1.25	Review of actions.
	Briefing on follow up actions (see below).
	Review of the Plan Improvement Process.
1.30	Close.

Stage 3: Post Plan Improvement

After the actual Plan Improvement session, it is suggested that you should follow up with the Account Owner. The actions that you might take include:

- Write to the Account Owner, thanking them for their preparation, complimenting them where appropriate, and summarising any particular actions that you think are critical. It is suggested that this be in email format, allowing the Account Owner to forward it to the rest of their team.

- Schedule a one on one meeting to check on progress against the agreed actions. If appropriate, this can be used as the deadline for re-submission of the (improved) plan.

- Ensure that the Account Owner has scheduled another Plan Improvement after an appropriate time.

Appendix 5: SWOT Analysis

SWOT Analysis is a very simple yet powerful tool that many people have heard of and may have used occasionally, however there are many interpretations of precisely how to use it.

	Good News	Bad News
Our Control	**S** Strengths	**W** Weaknesses
External	**O** Opportunities	**T** Threats

The academics all disagree over the finer points of SWOT, however to use it as a tool which summarises the overall relationship that you have with an account, then the following definition normally proves useful.

A **Strength** is a fact about the situation that is good news for us and is under our control (the control of the Account Team). Examples of Strengths might be:

- Good coverage of all managers within the IT function
- Josh Gilbert is a strong supporter of ours
- Great reference sites for their industry now available
- Track record of delivering projects on time
- Frame agreement in place with pricing that their Procurement Group have stated is attractive and gives us good margins
- Preferred Supplier status for all mobile applications

A **Weakness** is a fact about the situation that is bad news for us and is under our control (the control of the Account Team). Examples of Weaknesses might be:

- George Adams, Senior VP Sales & Marketing (a major decision maker) is openly against us
- No relationships of note outside of procurement or the technical group

- We have lost the last two major projects that were put out to competitive bidding
- Customer Satisfaction score went down by 11% last year
- Our on-site engineer has just resigned

An **Opportunity** is a fact about the situation that is good news for us but is not under our control (the control of the Account Team). In sales Account Planning we have to be particularly careful to not confuse Opportunities in the SWOT with 'Sales Opportunities' that we might put into our funnel.

Examples of Opportunities might be:

- They are expanding into South East Asia
- They have major issues with XYZ competitor
- Serious concerns about Return on Investment for current (competitive) systems
- Supplier rationalisation following merger
- Our corporate industry marketing group are investing in their vertical

A **Threat** is a fact about the situation that is bad news for us but is not under our control (the control of the Account Team).

Examples of Threats might be:

- Economic downturn
- Effects of their impending re-organisation
- Our product house being unable to supply working systems on time
- Our key competitor becoming more price competitive
- Instability in their management team

Notice that 'under our control' means under the control of the Account Team and reflects the fact that the people developing the plan can do something about it directly.

Appendix 6: VeloMore Organisation Chart

See Part 3 (page 69) for relating Case Study

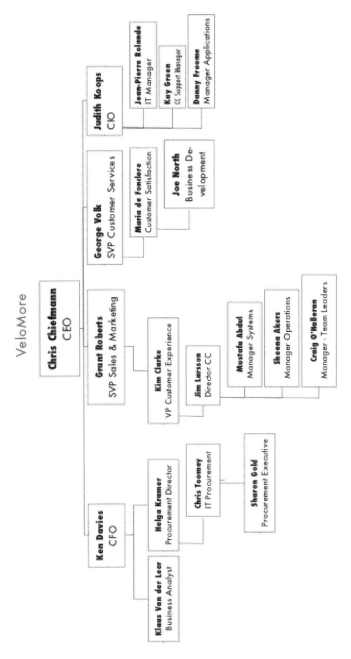

Index

About ProAct Business Development

Throughout Real Account Planning we have used materials, and examples from ProAct Business Development.

For over ten years ProAct has been providing sales transformation programs to clients in the complex B2B environment.

Since 2008 the approach has been updated and refined to take account of the New Norm of Selling driven by changed customer stances.

ProAct can deliver 1-1 coaching of Account Managers and sales leaders through to complete training programmes for thousands of sales people across the globe. Training utilises real workshops that focus on real accounts as well as a unique, high impact Sales Simulation to develop behaviours, experiment and gain confidence in new approaches.

For more information email info@proactbd.com or call +1 (800) 528-7759

About the Author

After graduating with a degree in Computer Science from Imperial College, London, Steve joined Burroughs Machines as a sales and marketing trainee. A brief period with Data General followed, after which he spent nearly ten years with Digital Equipment in various account management and sales management roles.

Steve then spent three years with Apple Computer setting up and leading their Large Accounts Division. He initially ventured into consulting and training in the 1990's before joining 3Com Corporation firstly as Sales Director for UK and Ireland and then as European Business Development Director.

Steve was one of the original founders of ProAct Business Development in 2001 and sold his controlling interest in 2008, although he still works very closely with the company and its network of fantastic coaches, consultants and trainers.

He still occasionally 'keeps his hand in' and recently completed a six-month interim management assignment with Avaya, being responsible for managing their UK business – an experience that he says was refreshing and taught him a lot.

In addition to training and consulting, Steve has written many articles and papers, and is a popular speaker at conferences and seminars. He is married with two children, lives in Bookham, Surrey in the United Kingdom as well as Abondance near Evian in the French Alps. He lists his hobbies as cycling, skiing, tennis, mountain biking and hill walking.

Steve can be contacted at steve.hoyle@realaccountplanning.com

Printed in Great Britain
by Amazon

56577191R00121